Finance, Sustainability, and the Climate Crisis

Also Available from Bloomsbury

The Global Minotaur, Yanis Varoufakis
Climate and Capital in the Age of Petroleum, Jeff Diamanti
Global Ethics and Global Common Goods, Patrick Riordan

Finance, Sustainability, and the Climate Crisis

An Incommensurable Alliance

Cengizhan Kaptan

BLOOMSBURY ACADEMIC
LONDON • NEW YORK • OXFORD • NEW DELHI • SYDNEY

BLOOMSBURY ACADEMIC
Bloomsbury Publishing Plc, 50 Bedford Square, London, WC1B 3DP, UK
Bloomsbury Publishing Inc, 1359 Broadway, New York, NY 10018, USA
Bloomsbury Publishing Ireland, 29 Earlsfort Terrace, Dublin 2, D02 AY28, Ireland

First published in Great Britain 2026

Series design by Charlotte Daniels
Cover image: Color square geometry painted in minimal urban architecture (© Artur Debat / Getty Images)

A catalogue record for this book is available from the British Library.

A catalog record for this book is available from the Library of Congress.

ISBN: HB: 978-1-3504-6939-6
PB: 978-1-3504-6943-3
ePDF: 978-1-3504-6940-2
eBook: 978-1-3504-6941-1

Typeset by Deanta Global Publishing Services, Chennai, India

Contents

Preface

This book addresses a pressing paradox of our time: the pursuit of sustainability within a global financial system built on relentless growth and profit maximization. Can these seemingly contradictory forces coexist? Or does "Sustainable Finance," despite its noble aspirations, ultimately perpetuate the very systems that drive social inequality and ecological destruction? I would like to share that this book is derived from my doctoral thesis, where I first explored these intricate and compelling issues. The research and analysis conducted during my doctoral studies laid the groundwork for this work, which has been refined and expanded to reach a broader audience.

This work argues that to fully grasp the promises, contradictions, and limitations of Sustainable Finance, we must look deeper than celebratory headlines and market-driven—or say, computer-driven—solutions. This is where philosophy—with its tools of dialectical logic and historical analysis—becomes indispensable. Dialectical logic allows us to cut through appearances and identify the underlying structural contradictions within the very definition of "sustainability" when embedded in the capitalist system.

We have been talking about post-truth for a long time. Without questioning the sources of information, especially due to the vast amount of information we get from social media, we take social media posts as true facts and correct information most of the time. The paradox is that we cannot distinguish what is false from what is true. But what is even worse is that the truth does not have any effect even when it is distinguished. True information is no longer important; it appears as just another feed in the ocean of information, taking its small place in the big data registry. It seems that this is one of the reasons for the growing apathy and indifference, new paradigms of submission to the ruling world systems. However, those who have the desire to seek what is true cannot give up just because what they are doing has no current effect on the transformation of society; they are not only torn by external conditions, but their desire also comes from within as they see, at least in minimal terms, what the setbacks and blockages are for such transformation.

This book is written with such an aim: to expose the dynamics of Sustainable Finance, even if there are not much actually promising dynamics for a rapid transformation of the system toward genuine sustainability. Drawing on the insights of Hegelian and Marxian dialectics, this work critically examines the historical development of Sustainable Finance, revealing its inherent tensions, and gradually expands to encompass the broader complexities of global financial markets, revealing the persistence of profit as the ultimate "essence" driving investment decisions, even those cloaked in the language of environmental and social responsibility.

Through a systematic and critical approach, this work seeks to demystify Sustainable Finance, both for those working within its institutions and for a broader audience grappling with its implications for a just and sustainable future. Key paradigms shaping current debates, such as the 2050 net zero goal and the push for "financed emissions reductions," are examined to reveal the often-illusory nature of their promises and the potential for these concepts to be co-opted by existing power structures.

This book does not shy away from the difficult realities of our current predicament. The analysis shows how financialization—the increasing dominance of finance capital over all aspects of life—exacerbates the challenges of achieving true sustainability. The drive for short-term profits and the inherent opacity of financial markets create significant obstacles to redirecting capital flows toward truly sustainable ends.

However, this work also seeks to go beyond simply diagnosing the problems. By incorporating insights from social psychology and biopsychology, the book explores new ways of understanding how individual behavior and societal structures interact to perpetuate unsustainable practices. This interdisciplinary approach, termed "biopsychopolitics" in this study, offers a more nuanced understanding of the challenges we face, moving beyond simplistic narratives of individual versus collective responsibility. Ultimately, this book aims to inspire a more critical and engaged approach to Sustainable Finance. It challenges readers to move beyond accepting market-driven solutions at face value and instead demand greater transparency, accountability, and a fundamental reorientation of our economic systems toward truly sustainable and socially just goals.

While acknowledging the magnitude of the task ahead, this work concludes with a message of cautious optimism. It highlights the potential for transformative change through collective action, drawing inspiration from historical struggles for social and environmental justice. By embracing the complexity of our current reality and remaining committed to the pursuit of a more just and sustainable world, we can begin to chart a path toward a future in which both people and the planet can thrive.

Introduction

Sustainability is a catchword that has become more common and relevant over time. It often means the idea of fulfilling the needs of today without harming the chances of future generations fulfilling their own needs. This idea, also known as the Brundtland definition, was first stated by the World Commission on Environment and Development in 1987 and has since become the most widely used and quoted explanation of sustainability. Sustainable Finance, meanwhile, is a term that describes the practices and principles of funding and investing that aim to help the shift to a low-carbon (even net zero carbon by 2050 or sooner), resource-efficient, and socially inclusive economy. This term, which came up in the late 1990s and early 2000s, reflects the increasing understanding and awareness of the environmental, social, and governance (ESG) factors that influence the outcomes and effects of financial activities and markets. Sustainability and ESG concepts are widely accepted and supported by governments, corporations, civil society, and academia as good and necessary goals for the welfare of humanity and the planet.

Meanwhile, 2023 was a year of extreme heat, floods, and fires that were worse than ever before. And it wasn't the first time we faced these disasters; they keep happening more often and more severely on this planet—the only planet where we know life exists while we search for signs of life far away in the universe. The truth is climate change is not something that will happen in the future; it is affecting our present. On one hand, sustainability is part of corporate social responsibility (CSR) and has ethical implications; on the other hand, it is related to profitability, the undeniable goal of businesses in a capitalist economy. Even though they pledge to cut emissions to "net zero" and spend trillions on Sustainable Finance, the global carbon footprint does not appear to shrink. And the so-called "carbon budget,"[1] as defined by the Intergovernmental Panel on Climate Change (IPCC) and which forms the basis of climate scenarios and pathways, is being consumed fast and steady. It means the probability of our planet facing irreversible damage increases each year. In fact, investments in "green" industries go along with the continued use of fossil fuels. How can Sustainable Finance support both development and destruction? What are the hidden factors behind this—factors that we miss when we only look at financial tools and measurements?

Everywhere there is talk about the great problems that our planet is going through: climate change, poverty, and the like. Until it was established that human beings had a direct impact on the degradation of the planet, climate change was supposed to be an act of God (or of natural law). Others, however, express doubts that humans have such an impact, maintaining instead that the influence of human activity on climate change is exaggerated. One of the foremost representatives of the latter group is the former—and perhaps the next as well—president of the United States of America, Mr. Donald Trump.[2] Let's not forget that Mr. Trump declared that claims about environmental change and the role that human beings play in it are deliberately overstated. He even pulled the United States out of the Paris Agreement, which was adopted in 2015.[3]

Climate change became a hot topic in finance after two major events: the Paris Agreement at Conference of the Parties (COP) 26 in 2015 and the Sustainable Development Goals (SDGs) adopted by the United Nations. Both events marked a broad consensus among many countries to address climate change. One might argue that sustainability is mainly related to the real economy, the domain of the producers of agricultural livestock, steel, cars, oil, and gas—industries that emit a lot of greenhouse gases. What does this have to do with finance? The easy answer would be "nothing." But this would ignore the role of finance and how it connects to the real economy. A more thoughtful answer, therefore, would explain how the financial system is inevitably involved because of its link to industrial capitalism. In our modern world, almost no company can invest in its projects or produce goods or services without credit. Credit is provided for such activities and operations. Therefore, financial institutions are presently and, for the foreseeable future, will continue to be directly involved in financing green—as well as brown[4]—projects.

This book uses "green finance," "environmental, social, and governance" (ESG), and "Sustainable Finance" synonymously, even though they may have some regulatory differences. All these terms share the same goal of reducing carbon emissions, despite their varying regulatory or legislative frameworks.

For instance, the European Union has its own taxonomy, a system that defines what is green, but a bank may not agree with the EU's definition. For example, nuclear power projects may be green according to the EU's taxonomy, but a bank may have a strict policy against funding them. In this case, what the EU counts as green may still be seen as "unsustainable" by a bank.

Behind the rhetoric and discourse of sustainability and Sustainable Finance lie many contradictions, tensions, and challenges that are often overlooked or ignored. How can we reconcile the pursuit of economic growth and development with the limits and boundaries of the natural environment? How can we ensure that the benefits and costs of the transition to a green economy are shared fairly and equitably among different groups and regions? How can we take into account the diverse and sometimes conflicting values and interests of stakeholders involved in sustainability and Sustainable Finance decision-making processes? How can we critically examine and challenge the assumptions and paradigms that underpin the dominant models and frameworks of sustainability and Sustainable Finance? These are some of the key questions and issues that I will address and explore in this book, drawing on the insights and perspectives of philosophy and dialectics. To fully grasp the promises, contradictions, and limitations of Sustainable Finance, we need to look deeper. This is where philosophy—with its tools of dialectical logic and historical analysis—is indispensable. Philosophy allows us to cut through superficial appearances and identify the underlying structural contradictions in the very definition of sustainability when embedded in the capitalist system.

One of the main arguments of this book is that Sustainable Finance, as an emerging sector of the global financial system, represents a crucial dialectical moment within capitalism. The pursuit of environmental goals through market mechanisms reveals inherent tensions between a profit-driven economic system and the preservation of the planet's resources. To uncover the nature of this dynamic, this book draws on Hegelian and Marxian dialectical logic to provide a philosophical lens through which to interrogate the successes and failures of Sustainable Finance while illuminating the path to a more profoundly sustainable future.

It is true that we live in an era where many say that philosophy has become less popular as other sciences have risen. However, the meaning of science itself has been changing for a long time. Especially in the last century, the supporters of the natural sciences have challenged the methods of the social sciences and the humanities. Because it does not use the empirical methods of the natural sciences, philosophy, usually seen as one of the humanities, has faced this critique. This situation has improved somewhat with the decline of behaviorism and the emergence of the cognitive paradigm. However, the status of philosophy in the field of the sciences is still uncertain.

Culture relies on philosophy, which offers a broad framework for thinking. Therefore, this study aims to demonstrate that philosophy, besides other roles, cooperates with other sciences, providing them with perspectives that they need to take into account. In the realm of philosophy itself, dialectical logic proposes a robust method that uncovers vital aspects beyond simple appearances.

Philosophers have studied finance (or money) as well. It is no coincidence that the writings of Karl Marx[5] and Georg Simmel,[6] as well as of John Maynard Keynes, on both pure[7] and applied theories of money;[8] and on employment, interest, and money[9] contain their own philosophical formations, views, and concepts. Many scholars from different fields still study and discuss these works, including their philosophical contents, because they research or write about money or finance. There are writings on the philosophy of finance, just as there are writings on the philosophy of many other specific topics. If our planet continues to have financial systems and instruments, it would not be surprising to see more books and articles that do philosophy about money and finance. In this study, I want to bring the field of Sustainable Finance into philosophy. My aim is to create and show what Sustainable Finance means from a philosophical point of view.

When we talk about philosophy, inevitably the question arises: What is philosophy? In our case, we must ask: What is the philosophy of Sustainable Finance? Rather than survey the vast literature discussing the essence of philosophy, I prefer to adapt and use Lyotard's question[10] in our specific context: Why philosophize about Sustainable Finance? This question makes more sense. Not only does it address what the philosophy of Sustainable Finance is; it also provides insight into the grounds for, and the fundamentals and the reasoning of, a philosophical approach to the topic.

I will now address the question: What is the purpose of philosophical inquiry into Sustainable Finance? Why introduce another philosophy among the many existing ones, especially when there is already a philosophy of finance? My answer is that I view Sustainable Finance as a process and an inevitable stage of capitalism, and I think that examining and developing this specific stage is a role for philosophy. One of the assumptions of this book is that Sustainable Finance emerged as a subcategory of finance. It expresses a conflict and a paradox within the category of finance itself. To uncover the essential structure of Sustainable Finance within capital—particularly financial capital—this study will explore the manifestations of this paradox.

The purpose of this book is to explore the historical and philosophical background of Sustainable Finance and ESG, and then, to analyze the challenges and potential of these initiatives, which seek to change the world through financial activities that focus on environmental (E), social (S), and governance (G) aspects. In harmony with Hegel's famous statement in the Preface to *The Phenomenology of the Spirit*, this introductory part does not go into detail about the conclusions reached, the objectives achieved, the methods applied, and so on. This book will examine and clarify how the transformation mentioned above occurs through the analysis of how capitalism develops itself; that is, the book will explain the development of financial capital by showing its own development.

Philosophical Insights on Science and Its Limitations

In this introductory section, I want to highlight the role of science in our world. People on our planet talk about science and how it benefits our species by improving our individual and social lives, how it makes our lives easier, and so on. Is this accurate? Or more specifically, is it always true? Have nuclear weapons really made life easier for us? Did a nuclear power plant improve life in Chernobyl? When we speak positively about science, we often reflect our desires and hopes, rather than the outcomes of scientific processes. We hope science will fully heal stress, disorders, cancer, and so on. However, we usually tend to overlook the methods that scientific processes employ and follow in pursuit of solutions. In other words, the science of our needs assumes the role of a liberator. This is why it is not surprising when someone commends science as a new divine force while confidently stating that he or she is an atheist or an agnostic. But such a statement is just as irrational as superstitious belief in occult forces. Science is a fact, a field; at the same time, opinions about its abilities, aims, and functions have a significant impact on wider issues. The difference between science itself and our expectations of science is therefore important, since any departure from a properly defined definition of the philosophy or ethics of science leads or can lead to harmful actions by engaging in dangerous inferences that are not related to the essence of science.

This situation, despite the controversy and debate it has caused, shows why the philosophy of science exists. Scientific codes of ethics, laws to protect human beings from the harmful experiments of the past, and to stop animal abuse in scientific experiments—all of this is connected to the role of philosophy and ethics. Philosophy's critical function, along with its dialectical logic and historical analysis, will remain an essential part of our lives for as long as our species lives on this planet. Dataism,[11] which is now presented as a new religion, reminds me of statistics, praised in the previous century as bringing salvation. One day, human beings will be able to achieve much more knowledge about what we call the mysteries of the universe, the puzzle of life; however, to celebrate every new scientific discovery as a messianic arrival—statistics, dataism—goes against the scientific method itself. It ignores the material life that relates to how human minds develop more complex and comprehensive knowledge and inventions. This is why philosophy will interact with the natural and social sciences, providing logical interpretations and assumptions, both learning from and contributing to them.

Philosophical Stance

Is it possible to have a common understanding in the domain of philosophy? One might say no. I cannot ignore the existence of philosophical disciplines. We have all learned about or seen for ourselves the increase and decrease of philosophical disciplines. The aims and functions of philosophy have sped up and multiplied these changes over time. For example, today, when we talk about phenomenology—setting aside Kant and Hegel, who used the term much earlier than Husserl, and even though Hegel's classic The Phenomenology of Spirit has the word in its title—we refer to it as a discipline that started with Husserl and progressed from there. But we also know that every famous phenomenologist created his or her framework by strongly criticizing Husserl, if not completely rejecting his philosophical thought. This shows, honestly, that divisions within a philosophical discipline continue; but, on the other hand, it is remarkable that this example shows that the evolution and direction of philosophy are similar to those of the natural sciences, as both involve falsification, criticism, and refutation.

There are two main branches of Western philosophy: epistemology and ontology. While epistemology deals with the theory of knowledge and ontology deals with the theory of being, these two fields have internal disagreements and external challenges. Philosophy tends to create different perspectives, so to avoid confusion, I will not cover all the relevant debates; instead, I will explain my own philosophical position and then give my views on epistemology and ontology. This will help the reader understand my approach to Sustainable Finance and ESG better. For this reason, I use part of the first chapter to explain the philosophical approach I have taken in this study.

This philosophical approach is that of Hegelian dialectical logic, specifically its "rational kernel," as described by Karl Marx.[12] For me, Karl Marx and Friedrich Engels are examples of successful successors of Hegelian dialectics. It is a pity that Marx did not manage to write the work dedicated to dialectics that he expressed a desire to compose. Marx's desire to write about dialectics in particular is first expressed in a letter dated January 16, 1858, to Engels, where he mentions he feels the obligation to write "2 or 3 sheets making accessible to the common reader the *rational* aspect of the method which Hegel not only discovered but also mystified."[13] Ten years later, in a letter dated May 9, 1868, he writes the following to Joseph Dietzgen: "When I have cast off the burden of political economy, I shall write a 'Dialectic.' The true laws of dialectics are already contained in Hegel, though in a mystical form. What is needed is to strip away this form."[14] In his letter to Dietzgen, Marx's intention seems to exceed the earlier two or three sheets; now it sounds like he wanted to dedicate a book or pamphlet to the subject. Most probably, we will never know his true wishes, but we can infer that he wanted to write about dialectical methodology in a way that would cleanse dialectics of the mystical form found in Hegel. Although Engels did not produce a separate publication on dialectics, he wrote about it explicitly.[15]

In this book, I want to show that dialectical logic is a valuable tool that allows us to go beyond the appearances that we generally take for granted, as if they were constant and unchanging facts. As such, dialectics can be applied to the fields of finance and its history to better understand the intrinsic contractions of the financial system and how they have evolved throughout history. I claim that Hegel did not deal with the harmful events that occurred on the planet and were documented in history, or he did so in a superficial way, examining them only in the realm of the mind. For Hegel, the Terror that came after and interrupted the French Revolution was a flaw of Spirit; he did not investigate its origins in and connections with conflicting forces of change. His system is one of rising and does not account for falling. For Hegel, the world, history, and Spirit always move upward, through contradictions. But now, we do not exclude the possibility of global breakdown—due to the damage to nature caused by human activity or as a result of the history of human action. Therefore, a wider and more critical approach, one that considers harmful outcomes, is needed; and this is found in Hegel's followers, such as Marx. I will explore this in line with either Marx's texts or his more general framework.

I state that my position is based on Marx's ideas for the method and approach of this book. I use the term "Marxian" because I may not be able to call myself a Marxist, even though Marx's thinking has always had an impact on me. The basic reason is my view of ideology. For Engels, ideology is spurious.[16] Marx and Engels had a negative view of ideology; I prefer to use the term "stance" instead. I argue that Marx revealed and analyzed the most important aspects of capital and showed a lot of evidence that capitalism causes poverty and injustice, and also that the growth of capital damages society and the development of the productive forces. However, I look at Sustainable Finance within the capitalist system and evaluate whether sustainability is possible given the link between sustainability and capital ownership. We have witnessed the rise and fall of what was called real socialism or communism in practice, and its outcomes. To me, this means that the Marxian framework needs to be reexamined, starting with a serious attempt to replace the old deterministic, predictive perspective with a range of possibilities, one that works by probabilities for the change and liberation of society. "Possible" means that something can happen, but not that it will happen. In other words, a world without classes, states, or dominant powers is possible, but it is not certain; it is only one possibility among others. To make it real, a strong theoretical framework open to practice must be established first.

Based on the above paragraphs, I ask the reader to remember two aspects of my philosophical approach: first, my Marxian interpretation is influenced by Marx himself, but also by Adorno's negative dialectics and concepts of non-identity. For me, Adorno is one of the most prominent thinkers who understood the spirit of the Marxian realm and its deconstructive and dialectical tools. Reducing the reception of the Frankfurt School to pure pessimism or elitism is excessively simplistic. Their complex diagnoses of societal malaise and cultural dynamics are still invaluable intellectual tools. We do not have to create a flawless system, and we should not pretend that everything is settled, only waiting for implementation. Please note, Marx mostly focused on the critique of the political economy of capitalist society in his works; he did not give much detail about how a communist society would look. For example, he emphasized that private property should be eliminated and replaced by collective ownership for the achievement of a communist society. But that's all! It is not the role of a critique to provide a perfect solution for this achievement. A critique should be sound on its own; it does not aim to rescue the world. It is a statement and a manifesto of what is wrong in our current situation. Only by recognizing what is false can we reach the truth. Second, non-identity can represent the Other; the Other is not absorbed into the dominant unity that subsumes the Particular into the Totality. Non-identity can represent women, oppressed nations, communities, and so forth. Fixed, determined interpretations of Hegel and Marx are not disasters only because they are wrongly applied; their underlying theoretical framework is also flawed. Therefore, this book also aims to speak for the Other, as Sustainable Finance, in reality, is the paradigm chosen by those who have the most—if not only—accountability for the climate issue.

In a nutshell, this book is about the investigation of sustainability and its inherent conflicts within the financial system, a system that traditionally relies on profit maximization and endless growth. These conflicts are not just accidental but are deeply ingrained in the financial practices that favor short-term profits over long-term ecological and social welfare. Drawing on the dialectics of Hegel and Marx, this analysis aims to reveal the structural tensions between the pursuit of sustainability and the requirements of a capitalist economy that operates under the logic of accumulation and expansion. By critically analyzing how these contradictions appear and are dealt with within the field of Sustainable Finance, the book aims to show the complex interaction between economic systems and sustainability goals. In doing so, it prompts us to reconsider the compatibility of current financial paradigms with the pressing need for real sustainability, suggesting a reassessment of what counts as rational economic behavior in light of environmental and social imperatives.

In light of the above introductory paragraphs, the book is divided into the following chapters:

Chapter 1—"Methodology"—outlines further the philosophical approach of this study. It provides the basic characteristics of Hegelian and Marxian dialectics, emphasizing the meaning of abstract and concrete and pointing out the role of immanence in the analysis.

Chapter 2—"Sustainable Finance: A Subcategory of Finance"—provides a definition of Sustainable Finance. This relatively lengthy chapter covers a set of important historical events concerning climate change and discusses their characteristics in detail. The chapter also defines the starting point of the analysis—a simple financing operation—of Sustainable Finance that will enable a move from the abstract to the concrete.

Chapter 3—"Sustainable Finance: Mainstream Concepts and Events"—builds upon Chapter 2 and defines Sustainable Finance as a subcategory of finance, a quantum that grows inside finance as a separate category. Dialectical logic entails starting from the simplest phenomena toward greater complexities, until the analysis leaves behind appearances. The method pursued is similar to that found in Marx's *Grundrisse* and *Capital*. Thus, the chapter explores in detail a mere appearance—among a myriad of them—of Sustainable Finance: a simple financing operation. That is, the analysis starts from the premises depicted by the mainstream proponents of Sustainable Finance, expands and explores the credit system and its connection to capital overall. On the one hand, it discusses the contradictory relations between Sustainable Finance and finance, defining what distinguishes them from one another; on the other hand, it lays the foundation for the further elaboration of how this contradiction-in-unity will develop.

Chapter 4—"The Limits and Inadequacies of Capitalism about Sustainability"—builds upon the previous chapters and discusses in detail why capitalism cannot achieve sustainability. It presents the targets of green finance transition, as set by regulators and international (or supranational) bodies. I claim that these targets are estimates heavily relying on disruptive technologies and are at the mercy of the hegemonic power of capital that can alter or even cancel them when necessary. Hence, this chapter also discusses crucial topics intrinsic to the financial system: access to financial information and knowledge, regulation versus deregulation, and financialization. It addresses the link between growth and financialization under credit money and argues that credit money exists in contradiction with industrial capital.

Chapter 5—"How to Achieve Better Sustainability?"—introduces a new term, biopsychopolitics. It discusses biopolitics and psychopolitics, as well as the unity and tension between the two. Moreover, it proposes that biopsychopolitics be assessed through the lens of dialectical logic in order to grasp the unity, contradiction, and dialectic between the biological and psychological aspects of society and individuals. This chapter also discusses social phenomenology focusing on responsibility. The chapter claims that sustainability, in its truest form, can only be achieved by abolishing all types of discrimination and by denying hegemony, including the hegemony of humans over nature.

Chapter 6—"Concluding Remarks and Future Tasks"—provides a summary of the analyses and premises employed in this study, concluding with remarks that address further developments that could be pursued on the basis of this study. The chapter draws a distinction between philosophy and the critical theory of society, proposing cooperation between these two domains, as well as with other sciences where applicable.

Notes

1 The IPCC is the United Nations body that provides assessments about the science concerning climate change. The body published its Assessment Report (AR) based on assessment cycles. The last AR published was AR6 for the cycle from October 2015 to July 2023.

2 Chris Riotta, "Trump Repeats False Claim there is No Climate Change Crisis as he Brands Science 'Fake,'" *The Independent*, March 12, 2019.

3 Roger Harrabin, "Paris Agreement: Trump Confirms US will Leave Climate Accord," *BBC*, October 24, 2019.

4 "Brown" is the term used for undertakings that are not perceived as green and sustainable.

5 Karl Marx, *Capital: A Critique of Political Economy*, vol. 3, trans. David Fernbach (London: Penguin Books, 1991). Part V of this volume is primarily dedicated to what Marx calls interest-bearing capital and credit money.

6 Georg Simmel, *The Philosophy of Money*, trans. Tom Bottomore and David Frisby (London: Routledge, 2011).

7 John Maynard Keynes, *A Treatise on Money, Volume 1: The Pure Theory of Money* (Cambridge: Cambridge University Press, 2013).

8 John Maynard Keynes, *A Treatise on Money, Volume 2: The Applied Theory of Money* (Cambridge: Cambridge University Press, 2013).

9 John Maynard Keynes, *The General Theory of Employment, Interest and Money* (Cham: Palgrave Macmillan, 2018). Keynes's works could be characterized as social and economic theory, whose premises mount a critique of the proponents of the classical theory of economics.

10 Jean-François Lyotard, *Why Philosophize?* trans. Andrew Brown (London: Polity, 2013).

11 The term is taken from Yuval Noah Harari's "Homo Deus" because it is a very good one that emphasizes the worship of data that is our truth, which is one of the main reasons for our common illusions. Yuval Noah Harari, *Homo Deus: A Brief History of Tomorrow* (London: Random House, 2016).

12 Karl Marx, *Capital: A Critique of Political Economy*, vol. 1, trans. Ben Fowkes (London: Penguin, 1990), 103.

13 Karl Marx, *Karl Marx, Frederick Engels: Collected Works, Vol. 40, Marx and Engels: 1856–1859* (London: Lawrence & Wishart, 1983), 249; emphasis in original.

14 Karl Marx, *Karl Marx, Frederick Engels: Collected Works, Vol. 43, Marx and Engels: 1868–70* (London: Lawrence & Wishart, 1983), 31.

15 Perhaps the most prominent example is Engels' unfinished *Dialectics of Nature.* See Frederick Engels, *Dialectics of Nature*, in *Karl Marx, Frederick Engels: Collected Works, Vol. 25, Engels* (London: Lawrence & Wishart, 1987), 313–642.

16 "Ideology is a process accomplished by the so-called thinker consciously, indeed, but with a false consciousness. The real motives impelling him remain unknown to him, otherwise it would not be an ideological process at all. Hence he imagines false or apparent motives. Because it is a process of thought he derives both its form and its content from pure thought, either his own or that of his predecessors. He works with mere thought material which he accepts without examination as the product of thought, he does not investigate further for a more remote process independent of thought; indeed its origin seems obvious to him, because as all action is produced through the medium of thought it also appears to him to be ultimately based upon thought" (Engels to Franz Mehring, July 14, 1893, trans. Donna Torr, https://www.marxists.org/archive/marx/works/1893/letters/93_07_14.htm).

1

Methodology

Theoretical Framework and Methodology

Every philosophical work inherently contains a methodological system of logic that must be consistently followed. This book is grounded in the theoretical framework of Hegelian and Marxian dialectics, emphasizing the inherent critical approach this tradition yields. My central methodology is dialectical logic—a mode of inquiry focusing on contradictions and the processes of change. Derived from Hegel and powerfully adapted by Marx in his writings on political economy, it's essential to understand how logic moves from philosophical idealism into a tool for practical analysis. To lay the groundwork for analyzing Sustainable Finance, I will first examine dialectical logic, then clarify the differences between Marx and Hegel, and finally outline the specific approach and method used in this study.

Dialectic

The dialectic is a valuable tool that can provide insights yielding a powerful critique of the world. The method by which the dialectic offers these insights is immanent; by dealing with inherent contradictions within an object itself, critical approaches develop organically from these tensions, rather than through externally imposed analysis. My contention is that dialectics supports science through observation, investigation, and the determination of stages—phases—and breakthroughs. In this way, the dialectical method informs and enriches a critical approach, ultimately helping us ask the most impactful questions, a fundamental task of philosophy. Now, to understand precisely how this analytical tool has been used for critiquing economic conditions, we turn to its employment by Hegel and Marx.

Dialectics in Hegel and Marx

Hegel is a towering figure in philosophy, known for highlighting the historical forces shaping human consciousness. An influential German idealist, he sought to show how thought itself develops throughout history. Hegel integrated religious concepts into his philosophical system, notably exploring the dual meaning of the German word "*Geist*," which carries connotations of both mind and spirit. For the English translator, it is challenging to choose between spirit and mind, as arguments for either could be made based on Hegel's original writings. I prefer to use "spirit" for the historical *Geist* implying a collective, historical agency; and "mind" for the consciousness of a single person or when describing individual minds. Though Hegelian dialectics held profound influence on later philosophy, I argue that their underlying idealism limits their practical application. In contrast, Marx inverts the Hegelian dialectic, grounding it in material conditions, a powerful tool for his scientific method. My method in this book takes inspiration from this Marxian approach.

The following two sections present Hegelian and Marxian dialectics in their essential aspects. This analysis will illuminate the crucial aspects of Marx's method that distinguish it from the Hegelian idealist framework.

Hegelian Dialectics

The intricacies of the Hegelian dialectic are famously complex, and a full presentation cannot be contained within this work. Still, a clear explanation of its main aspects is necessary to understand Marx's approach, as it serves as the foundation for my methodology in this book.

For Hegel, the mind was not a given and static thing. On the contrary, the mind is a dynamic, living unity that cannot be divided into parts or faculties. In Hegel's absolute idealism, almost every faculty belongs to spirit; and, for Hegel, our culture, habits, traditions, political systems, and the like are the realization and actualization of spirit in history. For example, Hegel might view the evolution of political ideologies across Europe as a manifestation of this historical development of spirit. However, this focus on spirit also reveals the primary difference between Hegelian philosophy and Marx's framework. Marx rejects this idealism, stating: "It is not the consciousness of men that determines their existence, but, on the contrary, their social existence determines their consciousness."[1]

Drawing upon this Marxian framework, it is clear that finance cannot be viewed in isolation but must be understood as a central element within our political and economic system. As a key social phenomenon, finance actively shapes social being. Hegel's focus on consciousness can't account for this. We gain clarity and a foundation for critical analysis by inverting the Hegelian dialectic—concluding that human consciousness ultimately derives from these material social conditions. Only then can we hope to grasp how issues like inequality, injustice, and social and individual psychological problems arise, even though consciousness retains the agency to resist and transform these very conditions.

Hegel's philosophical system aligns with tenets of German Idealism, like those espoused by Fichte and Schelling, seeking a holistic and fully bounded intellectual system. In line with this view, a speculative philosophical system must exclude nothing that lies beyond its self-defined limits. To illustrate this, let's look at a key idea from Hegel's *Science of Logic*: "The infinite—in the usual sense of the bad infinite—and the *progression to infinity*, such as the ought, are the expression of a *contradiction* that pretends to be itself a *solution* and an *ultimate*."[2] These concepts of the "bad infinite" and the "ought" deceptively pose as resolutions, yet they perpetuate a pattern of unresolved progression. To overcome this limitation, Hegel proposes "closing the circle," unifying subject and substance. Unlike their indeterminate state at the system's inception, this unity at the circle's close reveals concrete consciousness and determinacy. Importantly, closing the circle resolves the contradictions of the "bad infinite" but doesn't eliminate contradiction entirely. Instead, contradictions become drivers within a self-justifying process of intellectual development. Understanding this is crucial to grasping Hegel: The Absolute does not imply the absence of contradiction, but rather reveals contradictions and ruptures inherent within the whole system. To achieve resolution between these tensions and grasp the Absolute, Hegel proposes a method centered on dialectical thought and its unfolding within history as it shapes consciousness.

Hegel conceptualizes the dialectical flow as passing through significant transformations; what he would term moments—as breakthroughs—in the evolution of the Spirit. Each of them refines the Concept (*Begriff*). For Hegel, "The true is the whole. But the whole is only the essence completing itself through its development."[3] The speculative project remains incomplete if this wholeness isn't achieved. Thus, Hegel emphasizes the crucial role of dialectics, temporality, and history. Despite this appearance of a dynamic process, the foundation of his system in idealist thought ultimately prevents its full application to understanding material conditions.

What makes Hegel particularly important is his emphasis on dialectical logic and reason, which also develops intersubjectively in history. Whereas prior philosophy was often criticized for relying on isolated concepts of individual subjects or society without sufficient connection, Hegel's famous master-slave dialectic, also known as the dialectic of recognition, in *The Phenomenology of Spirit* emphasizes the role of intersubjectivity. This constitutes a breakthrough in the history of philosophy, one that has inspired not only philosophers but all those who reflect on the structure and development of society. Hegel was a pioneer in his criticism of the construction of thought and philosophical reflection on the basis of the abstract individual and society.

While Hegel's system contains inherent limitations—namely the suggestion of a preexisting consciousness and the overemphasis on spirit as the sole driver of historical formations (including society and the state)—his philosophical contributions remain undeniably significant. Not only did Hegel inspire both the Left and Right Hegelians, but his work also provided the groundwork for Karl Marx and Friedrich Engels' materialist reinterpretation of dialectics. Despite later criticisms, Hegel's influence extends to the Frankfurt School, Critical Realism, and even the recent resurgence of interest within analytic philosophy. One of Hegel's most enduring, though indirect, contributions to naturalistic and materialist philosophies lies in his emphasis on history. Most importantly, his prominence stems from the dialectical method, used to interpret the historical process as a progressive manifestation of reason, to quote Herbert Marcuse's apt formulation: "one giant realization of reason."[4]

While acknowledging the power of reason, Hegel's focus on idealism places fundamental limits on his ability to address material conditions. His emphasis shifts to speculation around historical evolution driven by teleological forces aimed toward an "Absolute" resolution. For Hegel, humankind's historical development accords with an underlying teleological logic—a system assuming an inherent purpose-driven progression within historical processes. In his system, a dialectical-speculative approach enables an interpretation of events in which "History mirrors logic."[5] He envisages, similar to the journey of self-developing spirit that arrives at Absolute Knowledge,[6] the "End of History" in which Absolute Spirit[7] emanates in the ideal state inherently riddled with contradictions. His notion seeks to resolve tensions between the individual and the broader collective whole but does not propose a state without any conflict whatsoever.[8] Thus, Hegel reckons that world development, progressing toward a purpose-driven "Absolute" along with the full development of individual consciousness, will culminate in a synthesis of these two aspects. Within his system, dialectical movement functions primarily as a process of Reason. While he references concepts like nature—e.g., giving the example of blossom[9]—the state, or intersubjective experience, Hegel ultimately views these as subordinate to the evolution of Reason, manifesting within a broader philosophical and historical framework. Importantly, his idealist emphasis on consciousness as preceding and determining social circumstances is where a materialist critique, such as that developed by Marx, finds a crucial point of departure.

Despite common misperceptions, Hegel did not use the term "dialectical method" or "dialectical methodology" in any of his works. For him, dialectics is the means to reach the Absolute through speculation; this is what makes his approach "dialectical-speculative" and allows us to call his philosophical system "absolute idealism" and "speculative philosophy." As Alan Norrie puts it, Hegel's *Logic* presents an account "of the movement from the understanding (the sphere of identity) to that of negative dialectical critique (negativity), and then onwards to positive, speculative reason (totality)."[10]

For Hegel, achieving the whole through knowledge was central, and the focus on spirit enabled this pursuit in his view. Yet, despite its contributions, speculative philosophy does not directly transform the external world of conditions—only how the world is conceived. While offering insights into thought processes, Hegel's work leaves a crucial gap: how we transition from pure analysis to transformative action within the concrete, material world. Marx confronts this head-on in his demand for philosophy to shift beyond interpretation toward enabling direct social and political change. Marx's famous eleventh thesis on Feuerbach captures this distinction and its implications: "The philosophers have only *interpreted* the world in various ways; the point is to *change* it."[11] Inherent in this thesis lies a fundamental separation between Hegel's philosophical approach and Marx's worldview. A truly transformational critical theory is necessary, in Marx's view, one that goes beyond Hegel and earlier attempts at understanding society to reshape it.

The breakthroughs emphasized above—namely, dialectic and intersubjectivity—while influential on Karl Marx, held crucial differences from how he would employ these ideas within his analysis of capitalist political economy. Another Hegelian concept, alienation (*Entfremdung*), holds profound implications for Marx's work. For Hegel, alienation is the alienation of consciousness from itself. *The Phenomenology of Spirit* demonstrates how this sense of separation can be overcome and unity achieved. As Marcuse highlights:

> he described the historical form of the conflict as the 'alienation' (*Entfremdung*) of mind, signifying that the world of objects, originally the product of man's labor and knowledge, becomes independent of man and comes to be governed by uncontrolled forces and laws in which man no longer recognizes his own self. At the same time, thought becomes estranged from reality and the truth becomes an impotent ideal preserved in thought while the actual world is calmly left outside its influence. Unless man succeeds in reuniting the separated parts of his world and in bringing nature and society within the scope of his reason, he is forever doomed to frustration. The task of philosophy in this period of general disintegration is to demonstrate the principle that will restore the missing unity and totality.[12]

Marcuse interprets Hegel as saying that we have become strangers in a world of our making that appears alien, and unless we can reconnect with and take control of this world—through understanding, reason, and action—we remain trapped in a state of frustration and unfulfillment. Philosophy, then, is not merely a passive reflection on the world but an active force that seeks to transform it. These concepts become more concrete in Marxian thought and the materialist dialectic, as we will see in the next subsection and throughout this study. Marx proposed praxis, the unity of theory and practice. I contend that this concrete schema has its roots in Hegel, who emphasized reason's development historically through human practice. In other words, Hegel never advocated theory alone; for him, too, practice was a prerequisite for the fulfillment of the restoration and achievement of unity between man, society, and nature. Thus, despite criticism, a practice focus for Hegel also offered essential context for his successor.

Marxian Dialectics

Though no single text provides a full and systematic outline of "Marxian Dialectics," Marx and Engels, through their numerous writings ranging from theoretical analyses to calls to action, applied a distinctive method of dialectical reasoning deeply imbued with a materialist lens. As this section unfolds, we'll see both the clear debt to Hegel's legacy and how their work significantly transforms both the content and intent of dialectical inquiry.

It's important to note that while often linked together, "dialectical materialism" is just one specific approach within the broader "materialist" philosophy. Materialism, at its core, simply means that the physical, material world is the primary foundation of reality. Marx and Engels speak of a "materialist conception of history."[13] It was only in later life that Engels employs the term "historical materialism."[14] Joseph Dietzgen was the one who coined the expression "dialectical materialism." Personally, I find the latter problematic because it gives the impression that materialism always requires dialectical analysis. I have encountered this misconception when I talk to some people I know in my daily life. Materialism is a philosophical worldview that can use dialectics when and if necessary. In fact, Engels refers to the "materialist dialectic,"[15] which is a more appropriate use—the dialectical tool *serves* the materialist worldview, rather than defining it.

Critics often label Marx's theories as deterministic, assuming everything in history is predetermined. The Marxian framework is rather relational and, far from being teleological, predicts that society would achieve freedom if social classes and exploitation were abolished. It is relational in that it emphasizes the role of material conditions and historical processes in shaping social relations and economic systems. It seeks to identify the underlying causes of social phenomena and to explain how different factors interact to produce particular outcomes. It is also relational in nature in that its focus is on the relationships between different social groups and classes and how they shape the distribution of power, wealth, and resources within a society. Thus, in order to understand social and economic structures, Marxian analysis often emphasizes the importance of understanding the true nature of these relationships that can be reached through analyses that go beyond appearances. On the basis of the interpretations of some Marxist thinkers and ideologues, this analysis is often accused of being deterministic. For me, although a classless society alludes to determinism, I would not argue that the Marxian system is deterministic. Critics of Marx largely miss the point that we are dealing with the second nature—the second nature in which human beings, as conscious beings, have appeared on the scene. The projections we make today may or may not become actual; our purpose in proposing them, as long as they are possible and plausible, is to show—philosophically—that they are real even if they are not actualized. This does not mean that they will become real, but if and when they do, our proposals would agree with the historical events that would follow. This, in a nutshell, is my interpretation of Marx, although I do not deny that Marx's conception of the progressive character of society is to a large extent inspired by Hegelian logic. Although Marx argued that capitalism would eventually yield to socialism, we should not see this as a foregone conclusion, but rather as a possibility that would require the conscious political action of workers and other oppressed groups to be actualized. For instance, one of the most influential thinkers of our times, Žižek, admits that Marx's conception is based on probability rather than on necessity; he still insists that it is teleological, culminating in communist society.[16] However, if we take a cue from Žižek's own analysis of Hegel's antagonistic Absolute, isn't it plausible that Marxist projections offer no such "final state"? Just as the Hegelian Absolute remains in a state of internal tension, a transformed society would still likely contain its own contradictions and possibilities for further change. In this sense, predictions become open-ended explorations of a better future based on historical evidence, not deterministic blueprints. This reflects my understanding of Marx's focus on the ever-present potential for change, driven by human choices.

How then should we interpret changing the world, as Marx advocates, beyond interpretation? Marx's eleventh thesis on Feuerbach does not mean that philosophers before him did not want to change the world. Otherwise, how would we account for Plato's Academy, Rousseau's social contract, and many other attempts made by philosophers and thinkers? For me, the explanation lies in the rarely discussed tenth thesis on Feuerbach: "The standpoint of the old materialism is civil society; the standpoint of the new is human society, or social humanity."[17] For Marx, the alienation driven by appropriation has not only an economic impact but also creates conflict within society: the class struggle.[18] The concrete need for change derives from this conflict. I contend that Marx is not denying former attempts to change the world; however, the change he conceives is a revolutionary, radically transforming society, abolishing the remnants of private property, classes, and so on. Hegel, in contrast, was the philosopher of civil society, and this liberal approach necessitates the existence of the bourgeois state. For this reason, Marx replaced civil society with human society, one where everyone can engage with each other without the need for a state that preserves private property, existing productive forces, and the like. Thus, in order to transform society and humanity, the entire system must change so that the world can change as well, and this is the task of the critical theory of society, with which philosophy can collaborate.

Marx fundamentally differed from Hegel in how he saw the driving force behind dialectics. By emphasizing the material conditions of society, Marx sought to strip away what he termed "mystical" components of Hegel's system. As he notes: "Hegel's dialectic is the basic form of all dialectic, but only *after* being stripped of its mystical form, and it is precisely this which distinguishes *my* method."[19] In his letter dated May 31, 1858, to Ferdinand Lassalle, Marx almost repeats this statement about the Hegelian dialectic: "This dialectic is, to be sure, the ultimate word in philosophy and hence there is all the more need to divest it of the mystical aura given it by Hegel."[20] On both occasions, Marx praises the dialectic as the ultimate form in philosophy and the Hegelian dialectic as its basic form. It was to this "eternal" character in Hegel that Engels also objected and echoed this view: "According to Hegel, dialectics is the self-development of the concept."[21] Hegel's speculative philosophy rests upon the evolution and self-development of history and the Concept (Spirit), whereas the Marxian framework maintains a position in which dialectics embraces social transformation through human action (praxis).

Engels' letter to Conrad Schmidt constitutes one of the most striking pieces of evidence of the difference between Marxian and Hegelian dialectics. Schmidt was an intellectual interested in Hegel and asked Engels how best to approach Hegelian texts. Engels, in his letter dated November 1, 1891, explains:

> The inversion of Hegel's dialectics is based on the assumption that it is the 'self-development of the idea' of which, therefore, the dialectic of facts is only the image, while the dialectic in our minds is but the reflection of the actual development taking place in the natural world and human history in obedience to dialectical forms.[22]

Through this distinction, Engels encourages a new focus—analyzing not the abstract ideal development, but how dialectical processes manifest within the material conditions of economic history. He notes the progression from commodity to capital in Marx's analysis, urging Schmidt to draw parallels with Hegel's concepts of being and essence.[23] Building on this framework, a core purpose of this work is to apply this dialectical lens specifically to the history of finance, unearthing concepts vital to understanding the development of Sustainable Finance.

Abstract and Concrete in Hegel and Marx

Moving from the idea of dialectics as transformation, as established in Marx's thought, let's now specifically address how the terms "abstract" and "concrete" are used in both Marx and his key philosophical predecessor, Hegel. "Abstract" and "concrete" are important terms to grasp in Hegel's system. Although there may be exceptions, if we hear someone talking a lot about the abstract and the concrete, that person is more likely to be a Hegelian or Hegelian-Marxist; with Marx, these terms are not used as much as with Hegel, because Hegel was more of a theo-teleological philosopher, although I am well aware it can be argued that he was not. For Hegel, and for Marx, a concept is abstract if it is separated from its context; it becomes concrete when its internal set of relationships is entirely revealed.[24] The beginning of the Hegelian system is the abstract unity of Being and Nothing, both indeterminate; it is only through Becoming that there is a transition to determinate Being. Abstract Unity is the most abstract, purest form of the Absolute. After Becoming's inception of determinate being—a thing with defined qualities—there comes concrete identity, the Absolute in its concrete, conceptual form. This involves a myriad of negations from beginning to end, each a moment in the process, and each the outcome of sublation (*Aufhebung*). In German, *Aufhebung* has two meanings, which, in English, require specification: (a) to abolish, to cancel, and (b) to preserve. In the Hegelian system, the movement of sublation is of the first importance, marking the emergence of a new moment that preserves some aspects of earlier stages.[25]

Within Hegel's system (and for Marxian analysis consequently), "abstract" and "concrete" hold specific nuances. My understanding aligns with scholars like Burbidge and Magee, holding that an "abstract" perspective offers an incomplete or simplified view. Glen Alexander Magee observes that, for Hegel, "abstract" and "concrete" are not categories in his system of logic, but descriptive terms.[26] Burbidge seems to have a similar interpretation,[27] stating that "abstract" and "concrete" are relative terms for Hegel: "So the logic is abstract when compared to the full life of spirit, but within the logic an abstracted universal can be distinguished from a concrete totality that integrates a diverse complexity."[28] For the purposes of this book, the key understanding is this: immediate perceptions remain abstract, while the "essence" of a concept or situation achieved through rigorous analysis represents its "concrete" reality.

The dialectical quest to move beyond appearances toward "essence" unifies both Hegel and Marx's analyses in their own particular paths. Hegel, in his *Science of Logic*, begins with the Absolute Idea in its purest, most abstract form (Pure Being), and his system progresses through a series of interconnected spheres ("Circle of Circles"), with each step adding layers of complexity, culminating in the concrete Absolute. This dynamic mirrors Marx's approach to economic analysis and history, where the "abstract" commodity form reveals its "concrete" essence as capital through a process of analyzing internal contradictions. Marx states, "The concrete is concrete, because it is a combination of many objects with different destinations, i.e., a unity of diverse elements."[29] For Marx, "the concrete" is a complex network of relations, ever evolving and incorporating seemingly disparate elements into a unified but dynamic whole. Throughout this book, the fragments and examples given seek the concrete within the complex financial structure of the current world system; when we reach the concrete, we will be able to grasp what Sustainable Finance as a paradigm means.

Social Ontology and Social Epistemology

Examining the very nature of social concepts (ontology) and how knowledge about them is shaped and justified (epistemology) is crucial for a deeper understanding of my work. Therefore, through an ontological examination, I intend to uncover the changing social meaning of Sustainable Finance and sustainability ideals within capitalism's historical evolution. For example, analyzing past legislation and asset types alongside current Sustainable Finance initiatives is critical for truly understanding how stakeholders like investors and bond issuers define these concepts today. Ultimately, this approach can demystify financial tools for the "common person," revealing how global economic forces directly impact individuals, even those who never invest directly.

This subheading shifts the focus to fundamental philosophical questions: What is the underlying nature of Sustainable Finance as a social construct (ontology), and how is valid knowledge about it determined (epistemology)? While my work is anchored in the empirical realities of financial practices and historical shifts, the philosophical lenses of ontology and epistemology provide the essential tools for interpreting the deeper meaning of concepts like "sustainability" within the capitalist system. This critical inquiry seeks to illuminate not only the current social function of Sustainable Finance but also its evolving definitions among practitioners in the field. In this way, I aim to provide a framework for broader audiences to grapple with the implications of these financial tools within contemporary economic and sociopolitical structures.

Ontology can make the hidden apparent. In the case of financial assets, efforts should be directed to finding out, for example, what the main driver is for the issuance of a green bond from the perspective of a bank. Epistemology might tell us, for instance, that a bond issued in accordance with the EU's taxonomy qualifies as a green asset. However, this may not be enough for a better environment or for society to achieve a better quality of life. Those who have the capacity and power to invest in such assets may become richer, but the purpose of the bond may be too limited to bring about social transformation. In such a case, the asset may indeed qualify as a green one; however, the financial institution issuing the bond may enjoy profits, and investors may have the benefit of adequate returns, even as there is nothing new under the sun in terms of environmental or social change. Thus, while an ontological lens helps uncover potential contradictions between stated aims and social outcomes, we must turn to epistemology for solutions. Marx and Engels rightly note the limits of pure speculation:

> Where speculation ends, where real life starts, there consequently begins real, positive science, the expounding of the practical activity, of the practical process of development of men. Empty phrases about consciousness end, and real knowledge has to take their place.[30]

Building on this insight, understanding Sustainable Finance in depth (epistemology) allows for true critique, and this can be a pathway to meaningful action rather than the hollow language of sustainability. I classify and discuss Sustainable Finance under finance capital, in connection with credit money and finance. Since epistemology and ontology are complementary, my aim is first to provide a solid foundation in the epistemology of Sustainable Finance, and then provide ontological insights. Without a solid knowledge of the topic, both its meaning and the consciousness of it remain inadequate.

The Role of Immanence

Immanence and immanent critique are indispensable to dialectics and dialectical logic because they enable us to comprehend the contradictions and the potentials within the extant reality, without relying on external or transcendent norms or ideals. Immanence signifies that the criterion of truth and value is inherent to the object of inquiry, and not imposed from outside. Immanent critique signifies that the critique of a phenomenon arises from its own internal tensions and inconsistencies,[31] and not from a predetermined or abstract standard.

For instance, when Marx critiques capitalism, he does not appeal to a moral or utopian vision of how society ought to be, but rather exposes the contradictions and crises intrinsic to the capitalist mode of production, such as the tendency of the rate of profit to decline, the estrangement of labor, or class conflict. He demonstrates how capitalism engenders its own negation and indicates the possibility of a superior form of social organization, communism, which would surmount these contradictions and actualize the human potential that capitalism represses. In other words, the dialectical logic of immanence and immanent critique discloses the dynamic and historical nature of reality and impels us to transform it.

This book's approach is mainly based on the Marxian framework. My goal is to go back to the origins, to revisit the philosophical and political insights of the founders of the Marxian tradition, reevaluate them, and examine Sustainable Finance from this perspective.

Slavoj Žižek, promoting the idea of a "return to Hegel" after Marx, asked:

> how would our present state of things appear from this starting point? Again, what if Hegel allows us as a better (proper) understanding of precisely those phenomena which are distinctly post-Hegelian, which stand for what "Hegel couldn't imagine"?[32]

In this book, I use these questions, but I go back again from Hegel to Marx through negative dialectics. I take negation from Hegel, offer a critical approach to the study of Sustainable Finance, and then explore the link of Sustainable Finance to global capitalism. The goal is to understand Sustainable Finance through its own process, without imposing preexisting judgments.

Having mentioned negative dialectics, it would be inevitable to mention another important thinker: Theodor W. Adorno. Adorno, although often referred to, was an undervalued or disregarded thinker and philosopher—just like the many others who disrupt common sense and power. For me, he is the most profound philosopher of the twentieth century and the one who understood Marx best. Accusations and allegations about him, about his obscurantism, his pessimism, and so on, are not uncommon among those who claim to seek meaning beyond appearances. In fact, Adorno's negative dialectic is a tool that can help us in the twenty-first century. Instead of closing the circles and fetishizing the holy triangle of thesis-antithesis-synthesis, we need to use the thesis and antithesis process continuously, without necessarily claiming that we have synthesized both and arrived at the truth. We must accept the open-ended dialectic that should not seek a synthesized and yet abstract whole. Non-identity thinking is not a mere nuance; it affects our way of thinking from A to Z. Adorno's great emphasis on negative dialectics and non-identity thinking is not just a philosophical show or discourse; non-identity thinking and the emphasis on antithesis imply our view of minorities, the other, hegemonic structures, and ideological apparatuses. Critique has no obligation to bring the truth, whatever the truth may be. Critique negates the contradictions within the concept (not between two or more concepts). Immanent critique arises from internal contradictions and negative dialectics. If critique succeeds in negating, then its task is accomplished. Forcing critics to also offer a solution is a common ideological apparatus of hegemonic political powers in general—not only in the capitalist camp.

Let us quote Adorno's statement on immanent critique:

> The process is immanent: the internal consistency of the phenomenon—in the sense that this is to be developed within the phenomenon itself—becomes proof of its truth and the ferment of its untruth. The guiding category of contradiction itself is twofold in nature: that the works formulate the contradiction and, in turn, through such formulation reveal it in the markings of its imperfections; this category is the measure of its success,

> while at the same time the force of contradiction mocks the formulation and destroys the works. To be sure, an immanent method of such nature assumes at all times as its opposite pole that philosophical knowledge which transcends the object.[33]

An immanent critique examines both what Sustainable Finance says it is and what it says it is not (what it tries to exclude from its area of accountability). This dialectical process—based on the Hegelian progression from simple to complex—aims to reveal hidden premises and how concepts like "sustainability" may be shaped in ways that preserve systemic conflicts.

Application of Methodology

Throughout this book, the methodology mainly strives to reach a greater whole through categories defined and negated—and preserved—in accordance with Hegelian and Marxian dialectics. When we look at mainstream textbooks, news, and documents, we see, almost without exception, that Sustainable Finance is a virtue-based type of financing dedicated to the sustainability of financial markets, the expansion of ecological investments, and investment in solutions for social issues. It is a special type of financing that will help decision-makers reach a carbon-free planet by 2050. To validate these claims, we need to first define the role of financing in history and how it evolved into Sustainable Finance, a trend of our own era. This is why we should conduct a historical and logical analysis, as Marx did in the *Grundrisse*, showing in the process the flow from commodity to capital.

Although the methodology for the analysis of Sustainable Finance is inherited from Marx's Grundrisse and *Capital*, the categories employed in this study will obviously be different from his. Marx dealt with Capital; this work deals with finance, and Sustainable Finance in particular. What we notice in the development of finance and financial capital is that it possesses its own immanent process which can be unveiled by dialectical thought. Throughout its historical development, financial capital aimed to maximize profit. Therefore, we need to first stress on terms such as "sustainability," "the sustainable economy," and "Sustainable Finance," and we need to then view sustainability from the perspective of capital and its owners. In fact, sustainability does not pose any threat to financial capital at all; on the contrary, it aims to create green capital quite in line with the effort at globalization. Capital owners need to maximize their profits; therefore, sustainable profitability should be in line with and even need to govern the other sustainability-related concepts. This true relationship between sustainability and capital should be kept in mind in all that follows.

We need, therefore, to discuss the current situation of Sustainable Finance to ascertain whether our historical analysis matches its present-day state. The relation between the promotion of sustainability and capital does not mean that the change advocated by the proponents of capitalism is merely a lie. On the contrary, they truly want to change the status quo, but they want a change based on their own rules and determinations, on sustained profitability and economic growth. The whole process and its projections depend on the design of financial capital and a financial system that supports that capitalization.

If we apply this perspective, we can see why the signatories of various initiatives are large banks representing dozens of trillions of US dollars. The commitment by the governments of developed countries to the Kyoto Protocol or the Paris Agreement, for example, reflects their reliance and cooperation with big corporations and banks. Developing countries will—*must*—rely on investments from the latter. Sustainability targets mean the free flow of capital without change of ownership.

The implicit character of financial capital and its advocates could be better understood if we turn to some concrete historical facts. Let us remember the case of the Pacific Gas and Electric Company (PG&E). This company is taken as a case study of how to ameliorate water depletion. Water, in general, is considered a raw material found in nature. This is one of the reasons why water is used in abundance and inefficiently. It is only when scarcity looms that firms recognize the increasing cost of water. PG&E has a very controversial history. The firm went bankrupt due to its liabilities for wildfires. Between 2014 and 2017 alone, the equipment used by the company caused more than 1,500 wildfires. As a consequence of the poor—or, say, irresponsible—use of this equipment, more than eighty-five people died in the fires caused. Almost 200,000 thousand people had to evacuate their homes. Here we have a process that began before the Paris Agreement in 2015 and continued until the company went bankrupt.

Was this PG&E's first terrifying action? No. Consider the following quote from the Energy Atlas website, which explains the violations committed by companies and the delays imposed by states:

> In 1952, residents of the town of Hinkley, California, alleged that PG&E knowingly dumped wastewater contaminated with chromium-6, a known carcinogen since 1925, into the region's groundwater. In 1952, the Pacific Gas and Electric Company (PG&E) installed a compressor station near the town of Hinkley in San Bernardino County, CA part of a gas pipeline system linking Texas to California. Since then, the company has used a carcinogenic chemical compound named chromium-6 as a corrosion inhibitor in its cooling system. The contaminated water was discharged into unlined pools, thus leaking to the aquifer serving Hinkley's residents water needs. The leakage occurred (at least) from 1952 to 1972, the year PG&E lined the discharging pools. However, it was not until 1977 that the California state passed a Law regulating the use of chromium-6 and limiting its concentration in water to 50 μg/L. In 1987, PG&E officials informed the state of California of high levels on chromium-6 in underground water north of the discharge ponds. The levels were 10 times greater than the limits established by CA's 1977 regulation. At that time, PG&E started buying properties affected by pollution. Yet, company officials told citizens the water was suitable for both drinking and agriculture.[34]

This sad story might already be familiar thanks to Steven Soderbergh's *Erin Brockovich*, the film that revealed the scandalous history of the small town of Hinkley, whose residents were exposed to grievous environmental and social harm. After much litigation, California became the first state in the United States to acknowledge and publicly declare that chromium-6 consumption was linked to cancer. A maximum contaminant level (MCL) for chromium-6 of 10 parts per billion (ppb) was then established by the State of California.

And what happened to Hinkley, California? As Mike Pearl reports,[35] it was almost deserted, the last shop selling beer preparing to close. This "unseen consequence" is exactly the focus of this study. Justice and regulations matter only if they are timely, implemented without delay. Justice delayed is justice denied, according to a well-known proverb, and it fits perfectly in this context.

The history of Sustainable Finance reveals that states and finance capital make multilateral decisions, engaging through the UN at the supranational level with treaties. However, experience also shows that such decisions are the product of their own needs, which are shaped by competition, reluctance, existing regulatory frameworks, and, most evidently, profitability and growth. We live in a world where even nongovernmental organizations (NGOs) help firms achieve profitability and engage with them through their profitability goals. Their purpose in aligning with them is to make them adopt sustainability. Sustainability is linked to profitability and growth, however.

As a concluding remark to this chapter, a preliminary mention of the inescapable and historical—and also logical—tension between industrial and financial capital is useful. This tension will be discussed in greater detail later, but I think it important to stress that there is always a contradiction and contest between industrial capital and money capital. Benefiting from cheap money is essential to the industrial capitalist because she or he wants to pay interest-bearing foreign capital at the lowest possible rates. The situation is wholly different for credit money and its owner: credit money should be provided at the highest possible rate to ensure higher capital accumulation. This fact has not changed since Marx wrote the draft of volume 3 of *Capital*. After the 2008 crisis, interest rates were reduced to boost the economy and growth. Three years later, Richard Dobbs and Michael Spence noted that the age of cheap capital will not last very long.[36] And this has been shown to be true today. What outcome can we expect now? A shortage of capital, diminished capital flow to emerging markets, and probably protectionism—remember the Trump administration's stance against imports from China. Dobbs and Spence's prediction was made in 2011, in line with the intrinsic capital flows of the world capitalist systems. Dominating markets through non-true, indeed dictated interest rates has to be reconciled with today's increasing interest rates and inflation. Signs of recession are becoming increasingly apparent, although the situation is not certain. Recession would not hit the United States alone and may become a global issue. We will soon see whether the Federal Reserve Bank and the European central banks raising interest rates will successfully keep inflation under control while avoiding recession. Either way, it is not difficult to perceive that money capital is prone to crisis—sooner or later, but inevitably. Understanding "sustainability" thus requires a thorough understanding of the immanent structure of the world system. It does not arise because of an ethical call by capitalists; it is rather a political economy that imposes it as a means to find solutions to keep profitability and growth at maximum levels.

Notes

1 Karl Marx, *A Contribution to the Critique of Political Economy* (Chicago: Charles H. Kerr & Company, 1913), 11–12.
2 Georg Wilhelm Friedrich Hegel, *The Science of Logic*, ed. and trans. George di Giovanni (Cambridge: Cambridge University Press, 2010), 120; emphasis in original.
3 Georg Wilhelm Friedrich Hegel, *The Phenomenology of Spirit*, trans. Michael Inwood (Oxford: Oxford University Press, 2018), 11.
4 Herbert Marcuse, "Beyond One-Dimensional Man," in *Towards a Critical Theory of Society*, ed. Douglas Kellner (London and New York: Routledge, 2001), 112.
5 Stanley Rosen, *The Idea of Hegel's Science of Logic* (Chicago: University of Chicago Press, 2014), 12.
6 Donald Philip Verene, *An Introduction to Reading the Phenomenology of Spirit* (Albany: SUNY, 2007), 8.
7 It is important to note that Hegel's use of terms like "Spirit" and "Absolute" does not imply supernatural belief as we normally understand it today. While some commentators emphasize perfection in his idea of the end state, within his idealist system, contradictions continue to exist due to the ongoing processes of thought.
8 Alexander Kojève, *Introduction to the Reading of Hegel: Lectures on the Phenomenology of Spirit,* trans. James H. Nichols, Jr. (Ithaca and London: Cornell University Press, 1980), 67. Kojève and others interpret Hegel's "End of History" as a state of resolved contradictions. In contrast, my approach aligns with scholars like Slavoj Žižek and Terry Pinkard, who emphasize the persistence of inherent tensions even within Hegel's "final" historical stage.
9 Hegel, *The Phenomenology of Spirit*, 5.
10 Alan Norrie, *Dialectic and Difference: Dialectical Critical Realism and the Grounds of Justice* (London and New York: Routledge, 2010), 52.
11 Karl Marx, "Theses on Feuerbach" [manuscript version], in *Karl Marx, Frederick Engels: Collected Works, Volume 5, Marx and Engels: 1845–1847* (London: Lawrence & Wishart, 1976), 5; emphasis in original.
12 Herbert Marcuse, *Reason and Revolution: Hegel and the Rise of Social Theory*, 2nd ed. (London: Routledge & Kegan Paul, 1955), 24.
13 For example, Friedrich Engels, *Karl Marx, Frederick Engels: Collected Works, Volume 21, Marx and Engels: 1867–1870* (London: Lawrence & Wishart, 2001), 94; and *passim* in the Marx-Engels Collected Works (MECW).

14 See Engels' letter to Conrad Schmidt dated August 5, 1890, where Engels uses the term for the first time and only to mention that it is a cliché. Friedrich Engels, *Karl Marx, Frederick Engels: Collected Works, Volume 49, Letters: 1890–1892* (London: Lawrence & Wishart, 2001), 8.
15 Friedrich Engels, *Karl Marx, Frederick Engels: Collected Works, Volume 26, Engels: 1882–1889* (Lawrence & Wishart, 2001), 383. A little later in the same section, Engels states that Dietzgen discovered this dialectic independently of Marx and him, and even of Hegel.
16 Hisham Aqeel, "Visiting Hegel at Dusk: A Conversation with Slavoj Žižek," *Rethinking Marxism* 32, no. 4 (2020): 459–66.
17 Karl Marx, "Theses on Feuerbach," 5.
18 Herbert Marcuse, *Reason and Revolution*, 290.
19 Karl Marx, letter to Ludwig Kugelmann, *Karl Marx, Friedrich Engels: Collected Works, Volume 42, Marx and Engels: 1864–68* (London: Lawrence & Wishart, 1987), 544; emphasis in original.
20 Karl Marx, letter to Ferdinand Lassalle, *Karl Marx, Frederick Engels: Collected Works, Volume 40, Marx and Engels: 1856–1859* (London: Lawrence & Wishart, 1983), 316.
21 Friedrich Engels, *Ludwig Feuerbach and the End of Classical German Philosophy*, in *Karl Marx, Frederick Engels: Collected Works, Volume 26, Engels: 1882–1889*, 383.
22 Friedrich Engels, *Karl Marx, Frederick Engels: Collected Works, Volume 49, Engels: 1890–1892*, 287.
23 Ibid.
24 See Abstract/Concrete in John W. Burbidge, *Historical Dictionary of Hegelian Philosophy*, 2nd ed. (Lanham, MD, Toronto, and Plymouth: The Scarecrow Press, 2008), 24.
25 Glenn Alexander Magee, *The Hegel Dictionary* (London and New York: Continuum International Publishing Group, 2010), 238.
26 Ibid., 30.
27 John W. Burbidge, *Historical Dictionary of Hegelian Philosophy*, 24.
28 Ibid.
29 Karl Marx, *A Contribution to the Critique of Political Economy*, 293.
30 Karl Marx and Friedrich Engels, *The German Ideology* (New York: Prometheus Books, 1998), 43.
31 Theodor W. Adorno, *Lectures on Negative Dialectics* (Cambridge: Polity, 2008), 9.
32 Slavoj Žižek, *Hegel in a Wired Brain* (London: Bloomsbury, 2020).

33 Theodor W. Adorno, *Philosophy of Modern Music* (London: Bloomsbury, 2017), 18.

34 Environment Justice Atlas, "Groundwater Contamination with Chromium-6 in Hinkley, California," https://ejatlas.org/conflict/hinkley-groundwater-contamination.

35 Mike Pearl, "The Town Erin Brockovich Rescued is Basically a Ghost Town Now," *Vice*, April 15, 2015, https://www.vice.com/en/article/xd7qvn/the-town-erin-brockovich-rescued-is-now-almost-a-ghost-town-992.

36 Richard Dobbs and Michael Spence, "The Era of Cheap Capital Draws to a Close," *McKinsey*, February 1, 2011, https://www.mckinsey.com/featured-insights/employment-and-growth/the-era-of-cheap-capital-draws-to-a-close.

2

Sustainable Finance

A Subcategory of Finance

Definitions are perhaps terms that can never be agreed upon. But they are very necessary because even a definition that is not agreed upon reveals the point of view and the starting point of the person writing or referring to it. In this section, I will first provide definitions of finance and Sustainable Finance. I will then outline the relationship between Sustainable Finance and finance by referring to Marx's analysis of finance. Based on these definitions, I will show how critical thought and action have approached ecological issues throughout history. History is a fundamental requirement: it provides us with time-related facts, changes, contradictions, and transformations. It is also a good guide and even a teacher. It is a series that shows that the thoughts and determinations we think are our own can be put forward long before us. In this way, we will have a bird's eye view of the history of opposition to finance from Marx to the post-Second World War period. This will allow us to compare with the mainstream paradigms in the following chapters and to establish a critical ground.

Finance and Sustainable Finance

There is more work to do before the conceptualization of Sustainable Finance. Since Sustainable Finance is a subcategory of finance, we need to further articulate the role of finance in a capitalist economic system before distinguishing Sustainable Finance and showing how it oscillates with the category under which it falls, a category that is itself the subcategory of a greater system.

In almost all aspects, Sustainable Finance follows the laws of the financial system's motion. Nonetheless, the adjective "sustainable" signifies a distinction. This distinction stems from sustainability's relation to financial activities that allegedly accord with the goal of a sustainable planet. In other words, since the political and economic structure included sustainability as a core trend, the domain of finance involved sustainability. There is an inescapable correlation between the economy and sustainable economy, on the one hand, and finance and Sustainable Finance, on the other. This requires closer examination. I first discuss finance, mainly as a credit system, before turning to Sustainable Finance more specifically.

Finance

From among the several definitions on offer, I take the following definition of finance as a reference point:

> Finance is the study of the management, movement, and raising of money. The word *finance* can be used as a verb, such as when the First National Bank agrees to finance your home mortgage loan. It can also be used as a noun referring to an entire industry. At its essence, the study of finance is about understanding the uses and sources of cash, as well as the concept of risk-reward trade-off. Finance is also a tool that can help us be better decision makers.[1]

The basic definition of finance concerns the raising of money and represents a movement needing management. This movement derives from a basic fact: one party finances (the First National Bank in the example above), and another that is financed. Money moves from the lender to the borrower. The suggestion is that both parties manage the process well: the bank—or financial institution—expects timely repayment at maturity, and the borrower should use the money borrowed for a purpose or a set of purposes—such as buying a house or paying tuition fees—and then repay the debt at maturity.

Risk-reward is one of the essentials of finance cited in these definitions. The lender lends money—credit money—to the debtor (the borrower, the industrial capitalist), and the money lent earns interest until maturity. If repayment takes place at maturity, the interest that the lender receives would normally be above the rate of inflation. A borrower would pay a home mortgage, for instance, in installments and, at the end, would own a house that could only otherwise have been bought with a lump sum payment.

In its simple form, finance is a relation and movement of money in which a lender enjoys interest-bearing benefits, and the borrower purchases goods or services that would normally be out of reach without access to credit. In this context, finance helps both parties achieve their individual targets. Those able to provide funds accumulate capital through financing. Those who need capital will attempt to gain money from a creditor (the lender) to be repaid over the longest term possible and at the lowest interest rate. Once this relationship is concluded, if the process works smoothly, both parties accomplish their intentions based on their initial targets.

Finance and Its Credit System

It is essential to locate finance within capitalism, but, again, there is no consensus. Nonetheless, to make my position clear, I will propose what I see when we talk about finance and its relation to capitalism overall. I believe it is useful to go back to see how finance and financial capital were defined at the time of industrial capitalism's rise, and then move to our own time to see how finance evolved in the history of capitalism.

Obviously, Marx was not able to complete his analysis of finance and the monetary system. Interestingly, he touched on these topics in the *Grundrisse*, The *Contribution to a Critique of Political Economy*, and in the first volume of *Capital*; all analyses remained incomplete and were not expanded further (the *Grundrisse* being the most comprehensive). We can thus sympathize with Engels's sufferings when he gathered Marx's fragments and struggled to assemble them to complete the second and third volumes of *Capital*. Engels did not try to hide the difficulty of the task in his Preface to the third volume.[2] Yet we have more than enough information from Marx's arguments to perceive how he assessed finance as a credit system; there is no need for discouragement.

Marx examined the credit system in the third volume of *Capital*. The fifth part of this volume bears the title "The Division of Profit into Interest and Profit of Enterprise." After addressing the nature of interest-bearing capital, Marx discusses "The Role of Credit in Capitalist Production" in Chapter 27. What he says continues to be important today as Marx distinguishes between money used for exchange and money used for capital accumulation. Indeed, money has historically had two roles. When we go to buy groceries or a cell phone, we use our money for exchange. However, the owners of a bank, for instance, use money to make more money, to accumulate capital.

This study does not examine capital and capitalism directly. Nor does it intend to discuss money and finance in detail. However, it is crucial to present money and finance and their relation to capital to indicate the position occupied by Sustainable Finance today in the domain of capital. For this reason, a brief presentation of the capitalist political economy is necessary. Money is one of the main concerns in life. We use it every day to purchase goods and services, to pay our bills, to pay our university tuition fees, and more. How does money serve? In its simple appearance, money is used for exchange. I pay money for a book; the bookseller takes the money and gives me the book. In this simple aspect, money is exchanged for a commodity (M—C).

When a producer of a commodity sells it on the market, the commodity has a use value for others. The producer does not create the use value of this commodity; it is produced for the use value of buyers. When—and if—a buyer buys the commodity, it has a use value for the buyer. If I produce a car and no one buys it, my car has no use value (unless I use it for myself). If, on the other hand, I start producing cars and there are buyers, then I receive money for each car I produce. Money, as the means of exchange, is used in every transaction. What determines the value of exchange? There is a myriad of products; many products fall under the same category, so how is the value of exchange determined? If I produce and sell trousers, determining the price at €10 per pair, this says very little. However, if I want to buy 2 kilograms of tomatoes at €5/kg, I learn that one pair of trousers = 2 kilograms of tomatoes. Now we have adequate information. We have a measure. Money is the universal measure. It represents an exchange based on quantity.

Exchange is the first function of money; it is used to acquire another commodity (money as commodity). David Harvey states that "the exchange of two commodities also presupposes a relation of equivalence between them and indicates an equivalent form of value."[3] Money is the *universal equivalent*[4] that represents this equivalence as a measure. Through the circulation of commodities based on the mode of production, the owners of the means of production accumulate more money. The examples offered above did not include the details of this accumulation. In fact, if I own an automobile company, my purpose is to sell my cars at a price that more than covers my expenses: some surplus value and profit. Surplus value and profit are not the same; nonetheless, and ideally for the capitalist, both should generate a higher return at the end of the production process. Who, in a capitalist mode of production, would want to sell a car at a price that only covers production costs and expenses? Let's say that I produce shirts and my costs—machinery, rent, labor, etc.—are €15,000. If I sell shirts at €18,000, my gross profit is €3,000. In other words, I make 3,000/15,000 = 0.2 x 100 = 20 percent gross profit. At the beginning, I invested €15,000; at the end of the process, I sell and get my €15,000 back, plus €3,000 extra. What do I do with this money? There may be innumerable answers to such a question. However, for the purpose of this study, I will use all this money for another production process. Now, my initial investment can be €18,000 instead of €15,000. I made money out of money; I added capital to my existing capital. This is what Marx called the *accumulation of capital*.

In the above account, we see a completely different function of money. It is not money for exchange only; it is money as capital. This is the second function of money, and it is essential for capitalists to own money as capital. This is what Marx brought to light. After his extended studies of the subject, he demonstrated, supported by copious information and strong evidence, that this duality contained in money is the essence of capital. When we study Marx and his works on political economy, it is important to keep this in mind: *money as capital*. Here again, we see how Marx expanded his analysis from the commodity (appearance—Being) to capital (Essence), rising from the abstract to the concrete.

Money as capital should be accumulated. Capitalists want this accumulation to continue ad infinitum! They want to invest a certain amount of money, and, after exchange, they want to have more money. This can be expressed in the following formulas: M – C – M' and M' > M.

Marx also revealed a hidden aspect of the production process. If everything were valued equally at the exchange process, how would it be possible that M' was greater than M? In short, he convincingly explained that surplus value arises from the exploitation of the labor force of workers; otherwise, surplus value would not exist at all. Surplus value signifies the labor time that workers dedicate—above the hours for their own household—to the owners of capital who exploit their labor: a universal fact that has not changed since Marx first unmasked it. Surplus value was concealed by political economists and capitalists behind paradigms, rhetoric, and other deceptions. Such capitalist abstraction is still strong today.

We can link the above summary to finance as a credit system. In one of the examples above, a shirtmaker invested €15,000 of capital; at the end of the process, this capital became €18,000. We will use this example to understand the role of finance as a credit system. We will assume that the shirtmaker lacks sufficient capital. The producer has only €10,000 in hand but estimates that shirts can sell for €18,000 in total, and that an additional €5,000 of capital is needed to cover the production costs. In this example, the producer needs €5,000 from an external party. In this case, the external party is a bank—or, more broadly, any financial institution. The bank grants a loan to the producer with the intention of receiving the credit money later, at maturity. The bank is not a producer of commodities, but it has money; it does not provide a use value for others through production but acts as an intermediary. It provides credit, lends credit money, and receives its credit money back at maturity. The aim of the bank is to receive a higher amount of credit money at maturity, which can be expressed as M – M' where M' > M. On the other hand, the following can be assumed for the shirtmaker: with €10,000 own capital, and €5,000 foreign capital (the bank's capital), the producer reaches a sale volume of €18,000. However, the producer pays interest to the bank together with and in addition to the credit amount. Let us assume that the shirtmaker pays the loan amount, that is, €5,000 plus €250 interest. In this case, compared to our initial example above, in which the producer made a surplus value of €3,000, the gain is now €2,750 (€3,000 surplus—€250 interest paid to the bank). The bank gained an interest income of €250. The bank may have provided this credit from its customers' savings accounts and likely pays interest on their deposits; however, this is a process internal to the financial institution and will not be dealt with in this study. Nonetheless, it should be borne in mind that the bank's net interest income is not the whole €0.25.

In this scenario, the situation is clear, but it is still useful to repeat explicitly that the circulation of money capital is M—M'; it is money accumulated through money itself. The relation to the commodity is indirect, through a borrower, and can be ignored from the perspective of the bank. Therefore, banks and financial institutions accumulate their money capital through their already existing money capital:

> As the subject of borrowing and lending in this relationship, money capital becomes a special type of commodity. It provides the use value of self-expansion for both lender and borrower simultaneously, the former realising the interest and the latter the profit of enterprise that remains, after the payment of interest, from the surplus value produced through the use of the borrowed money capital. Marx emphasises that the price of this unique commodity (the interest rate) is "irrational," since it bears no relation to any underlying production conditions. It depends entirely upon the competitive relations between borrowers and lenders.[5]

There is indeed a link between money and finance. Apparently for this reason, Marx employed interest and interest-bearing capital as essential categories in his analyses. He rightfully stated that the twin brother of interest-bearing capital is merchant capital, which was on the scene long before the capitalist mode of production.[6] In fact, merchant capital resembles the credit flow in modern capitalism since "The merchant borrows money to make a profit with it, to use it as capital, i.e., to lay it out."[7] The process is the same as in the example of the shirtmaker who borrowed money from the bank and repaid the loan at maturity together with the interest accrued. The important point here is to keep in mind that money, through exchange relations, involves itself as an external factor independent of production (M—M'). By gaining interest from money, interest-bearing capital grows. Marx also observes, based on his historical analysis, that usurer's capital is the archaic form of interest-bearing capital:

> This violent struggle against usury, the demand for the subjection of interest-bearing capital to industrial capital, is simply the prelude to the organic creations that these conditions of capitalist production produce in the form of the modern banking system, which on the one hand robs usurer's capital of its monopoly, since it concentrates all dormant money reserves together and places them on the money market, while on the other hand restricting the monopoly of the precious metals themselves by creating credit money.[8]

This explains how modern banking absorbed usurers' credit in its own favor while preserving its mechanism—a very good example of Hegel's *Aufhebung*.

Marx also mentions that "the *credit system* is its own creation and is itself a form of industrial capital"[9] that "originally is a *polemical form* directed against the old-fashioned usurers (goldsmiths in England, Jews, Lombards, and others)."[10] What should be understood is that whatever its roots, the credit system is a form of financial capital.

Historically, merchant's capital was a form of money. Money was used as a medium of exchange. Money was the universal equalizer used in the quantification (value) and pricing of commodities. Money was also a commodity. However, when explaining and analyzing interest-bearing capital, Marx defines the role of money as money as capital. His analysis is based on lending and borrowing, that is, the system of credit between the owners of money capital and the industrial and/or merchant capitalists.

For Marx, the use of credit is essential. When talking about interest, we observed that the mere act of borrowing from a creditor and paying interest at maturity does not automatically qualify as interest-bearing capital. This type of borrowing took place before the advent of industrial capitalism. However, the use of credit distinguished merchant's and industrial capital. Credit should be used for the circulation of industrial capital, thus allowing the funding advanced to become money capital. This is what Marx emphasizes. In other words, when we talk about interest-bearing capital, we are talking about modern capitalism—modern, that is, in the sense used by Marx.

What took place after the circulation of interest-bearing capital? We can give a simple answer to that question: a new class was born! This class consisted of money capitalists. And what happened when this class was born? The answer is again simple, but its consequences are rather tragic: money capitalists "control the social power of money and . . . are sustained out of interest payments."[11]

Fictitious Capital: Tension between the Imaginary and the Real

Another important point merits mention: fictitious capital. In our example of the shirtmaker who borrowed money from the bank, we assumed that the bank kept its money capital ready to be used by the industrial capitalist. In most cases, this availability stems from the flexibility of money capital. When money is capital, it is more dynamic and mobile. However, while its flexible nature renders it independent, it cannot stray far from industrial capitalism. As a result, in some cases, money capitalists provide loans to industrial capitalists, meaning that the loan money loses its flexibility for a certain period as it cannot be used elsewhere.

In our example of shirt production, money was loaned to produce shirts. The bank may find another lending opportunity, but due to the loss of flexibility, it cannot take advantage of it because of the lack of funds. Money lent to the shirtmaker entails a loss of flexibility of the bank's money capital. This impediment is overcome by what Marx called fictitious capital.

Let us reconsider the example of the shirtmaker. The producer received credit from the bank for the purpose of selling shirts, which would then allow him to repay the loan amount plus interest to the bank at maturity. However, the producer acquired money from the bank but did not sell any shirts at the start of the process. With the money borrowed, the producer should either buy machinery for production, hire a labor force, or do anything necessary for production or sale. The bank has a loan agreement or some collateral over the product—paper—and intends for its money be repaid.

For Marx, the value represented by paper has a fictitious value. However, the bank can sell this value in secondary markets and circulate it as though it were credit money. So, though unrealized and fictitious, value initiates circulation. This represents a serious contradiction between credit money and commodity money. This is where the financial system makes its profits and accumulates capital; real money, on the other hand, follows its own initial route. This provides a clue as to how financial crises can arise from the circulation of fictitious money.

At its inception, the credit system, or, say, the financial system may not aspire to be more than an assistant that collects (deposits) and distributes (credit) money. However, because of the immanent nature of money capital, it grows into a giant that controls and centralizes capital. Marx quotes the following from William Leatham, a Yorkshire banker: "In times of abundance and cheap money this [fictitious capital] I know reaches an enormous amount."[12] This is an inescapable fact, both historically and in contemporary terms, when capital is accumulated by a "gigantic" minority. Due to this enormous, inevitable growth with great social—socially *detrimental*—impacts, it is unsurprising that Rudolf Hilferding and Vladimir Lenin spoke of the era of imperialist finance capital.

Sustainable Finance

Now that the philosophical ground, method, and framework have been presented, let us focus on the history of Sustainable Finance before undertaking its analysis. First, I will provide the definition of Sustainable Finance.

Normally, it is useful to provide an account of the subject under study. A difficulty arises in the case of Sustainable Finance or Green Finance, which, as with finance, has no agreed-upon definition. Nonetheless, it is still important and necessary to provide such a definition and thus delineate the subject under consideration in this work. From the several definitions currently proposed, I choose the one provided by the European Commission (EC), which covers the core common points:

> "Sustainable Finance" generally refers to the process of taking due account of environmental and social considerations in investment decision-making, leading to increased investments in longer-term and sustainable activities. More specifically, environmental considerations refer to climate change mitigation and adaptation, as well as the environment more broadly and related risks (e.g. natural disasters). Social considerations may refer to issues of inequality, inclusiveness, labour relations, investment in human capital and communities.[13]

The above definition defines Sustainable Finance as an investment in long-term, sustainable activities that take into account environmental and social challenges. In this context, ESG and sustainability can be used interchangeably. The primary elements are the environment and social factors, and governance is required to carry them out. Sustainable Finance is a form of funding that enables investments to combat climate change, inequality in society, and other significant issues.

As the EC's definition implies, Green or Sustainable Finance attempts to implement decisions that include environmental and social aspects. For instance, mitigation against climate change and coverage against natural disasters fall into this category. In fact, any investment that pays attention to matters of inequality, communities, human capital, and the like counts as "social."

Green bonds are one of the typical products of Sustainable Finance. Roman Berrou et al. call them the most advanced product.[14] Sustainable Finance is similar to the simple form of the main mechanism of finance, provided that the financing is done for specific and limited aims that address ecological or social concerns. Rather than financing for general purposes, it engages with matters of sustainability, as in the case of environmental and social issues. For instance, when a contractor builds houses as part of a sustainability project, whether social or eco-friendly housing, the bank's financing qualifies as sustainable lending activity.

As is clear from the definitions above, the parties involved in simple financing, in both regular and sustainable forms, are the same: the Lender (usually a financial institution, a bank) and the Borrower (usually a corporation). The difference is that Sustainable Finance applies financing more narrowly, namely, for environmental or social purposes.

Sustainability Ratings: A New Measure

Not much is explained by a simple Sustainable Finance transaction. For example, it only includes a creditor and a debtor, and when the transaction ends, it disappears. But there is more to it than just appearing to exist. Pricing is important in the financial industry and requires accurate implementation. This requires making the right credit risk decision. We need something quantitative to properly assess credit risk. Qualitative methods are still important in some areas, but there is a need for quantification. Credit rating provides this quantification. Rating is the quantification of the quality of the risk. It is therefore a measure that transforms the original qualitative concept of risk into a quantitative one. Sustainable Finance needs to be quantified and measured through ratings, just like the financial system itself. At the moment, qualitative approaches are still important, but sustainability ratings (ESG ratings) are becoming more and more of a standard and will soon lead to the dominance of the quantitative approach. There are already a number of providers of sustainability ratings, including Sustainalytics, Moody's,[15] and Morgan Stanley Capital International (MSCI). Their published ratings are not only used or referenced by credit providers (banks); they are also taken into account by individual and institutional investors—another aspect to consider from the perspective of financialization.

The quality is provided in the definition of Sustainable Finance, the quantity is a single loan, and the measure is the ESG rating, which is based on the assessment and classification of ESG-relevant factors. In a single transaction, once the company repays the loan, the cycle disappears and vanishes. Nonetheless, the measure—the rating—enables us to observe changes in quantities; some grow—as a consequence of their implementation of ESG as measured by ratings—while others disappear due to poor ratings (indicating that these companies have not implemented ESG). This contradiction reveals the oscillation between ESG compliance and ESG unawareness, resulting in access or non-access to credit, respectively. In financial systems, circulation is essential. A system cannot be sustained by one-time transactions or relationships. Why do banks and their customers meet in the realm of finance? More details are needed to understand it. There still remains a lack of information that ought to clarify how circulation works. When banks lend money, they earn interest. When they issue and sell securities, they usually earn commissions. Both are profits for the bank. When a company borrows money, its purpose is to sell products at a price higher than its cost of production and thus make a profit. When both parties benefit from their financial relationship, they will come together again because they will see this relationship as a means to grow and benefit. Credit and production need one another and reinforce one another.[16] Without this circulation, profit and growth would not be explained sufficiently. In order to run circulation in compliance with ESG norms, rating (measure as discussed) is essential.[17]

Sustainability as Appearance, Profit as Essence

For the financial system, including Sustainable Finance, profit is essential. The goal of Sustainable Finance advocates is to persuade investors that the profitability of ESG investments is as high as that of other investments. Such promotion clearly emphasizes profitability, rather than the virtues of a green planet. The goal is to continue to remain profitable in the long run, sustainably. If banks or companies have no profit, they have no interest in sustainability: the dark side of the moon. Sustainable Finance's analysis of phenomena began with appearances as parts of being. Yet appearances, in their immediacy, cannot fully represent essence and are almost always abstract. Almost nothing is what it seems. As Marx states, "all science would be superfluous if the form of appearance of things directly coincided with their essence."[18] Beyond the simple transactions above, there is a need for an examination of the other components of the subject matter. Beyond the simple transactions presented above, we need to find out and see what brings parties into transactions with each other. When we look at these other constituents, we see that the transaction process is not free. Some criteria must first be met. Firms are required to be financially creditworthy and also need to demonstrate that they have sufficient investments and a willingness to transform to achieve a green planet.

The requirements of the financial system, such as creditworthiness and sound financial statements, are part of Sustainable Finance. Furthermore, specifically for this subset, a company needs to demonstrate its commitment to sustainable business practices, with due attention to environmental (E) and social (S) considerations, and with good governance (G). In other words, companies must be measured in order to determine whether they can enter the realm of Sustainable Finance. This is done by measuring the company's sustainability rating. In general, a credit rating is a measure of a company's financial health, but a sustainability rating is a measure of a company's compliance with sustainability criteria. For a company to operate in the market, both ratings must be favorable; if they are not, then any failure would affect the company's profitability and prevent it from transacting with market participants and generating profits and growth. Without making a profit, no business can survive in the capitalist system. In fact, in the above scenario, money capital is accumulated (as interest-bearing capital). What now appears is that the bank made a loan in order to receive a larger amount of money upon repayment. That is, the main purpose of the bank is first to accumulate money capital, and this accumulation can be achieved by lending money or earning commissions.

The essence of Sustainable Finance, as with finance in general, is profit. Recognition of this fact is necessary for the understanding of Sustainable Finance. Sustainable Finance, in the main, nourishes the owners of capital and seeks to generate more profit for its companies. As a result, it becomes clear that the primary purpose of sustainability and Sustainable Finance is not to combat climate change, but to save the hegemonic position of capital through the "green" conversion, which is now quite dubious, given that it is at the mercy of finance capital.

Excursus: The Concept of Sustainability in History

The history of Sustainable Finance can be traced back to the late seventeenth century when religious groups advocated the concept of responsible investment. Quakers opposed investments in gambling, tobacco, and later, in the slave trade. Henry Cadbury[19] refers to the 1688 Germantown Protest, published in 1844, as the first document of social responsibility. John Wesley's Methodist sermon, "The Use of Money" (1760), called for the responsible use of money.[20] Thus, the roots of socially responsible investing (SRI) are almost as old as investing itself, and it is not surprising to see that religious communities were the pioneers in making an ethical call. What we can state on the basis of these historical facts is that Sustainable Finance has its origins in an ethical perspective of socially responsible investment. We can also observe that environmental issues were not of great concern in earlier centuries, whereas social issues like slavery and injustice dominated. In other words, the "social" in ESG prevailed over the "environmental." The term "responsibility" was used in relation to social impact.

The ethical call for the proper use of money distinguished different investment purposes. This demonstrates that Methodists were engaged in the development of the monetary system of the eighteenth century. This is, moreover, a striking example that affords insight into the difference between wealth and capital. Wealth and capital are not identical things. One's own or foreign wealth is necessary for capital, but wealth can exist without capitalization. As such, wealth is a condition for capital. Only if it is not used for production and the like can one talk only of wealth without capital (in Marxian terms). If wealth is used for investment, it gains approval in the Methodist framework; if it is not, it is cursed. This is one of the hidden aspects of capital. Today, in countries where deposits—including commodity deposits such as interest-bearing gold—are not great, it is not surprising to see governments call on the common people to deposit the money they keep "under the mattress," or other wealth, such as gold, in the banks. A good example is the president of Turkey who, in many speeches, has encouraged citizens to invest by depositing their wealth. "Idle" or unused wealth does not obey the market imperative. For this reason, it is cursed. It does not deliver capital that can be used for further investments in the system. Financial institutions need deposits so that they can lend money and exploit the margin spread between what they borrow from their customers and the loans they give to others. If no money is invested in bonds or funds, then banks, brokers, and financial institutions cannot make any commission. Let us now look at the historical development of environmental concerns.

Was Marx Really Indifferent to Ecology?

Environmentalists and scientists who have warned about the dangers of greenhouse gases (GHGs) since the early twentieth century, including Svante Arrhenius, first proposed the idea that human activity caused global warming in the 1890s. Arrhenius's 1896 "On the Influence of Carbonic Acid in the Air upon the Temperature of the Ground" is considered to be the first scientific study to quantitatively demonstrate the potential of human activity to cause global warming. Arrhenius calculated the effects that different concentrations of carbon dioxide (CO_2) in the atmosphere had on the Earth's temperature, using the concept of radiative forcing. He found that doubling the concentration of CO_2 in the atmosphere could increase global temperatures by 5°C–6°C, a prediction that has been borne out by later scientific research.

Yet, some decades before Arrhenius, we can see that environmental and social issues were important to Marx and Engels. I am not arguing that Marx and Engels were ecologists; in their era, clearly, no one was. What I am arguing is that they were not insensitive to the issue in relation to their own time. If someone were to pose the reasonable question, "What might Marx and Engels have to say to us about ecology today?" I would speculate that they would stress the importance of ecology and link it to global capitalism's principle of profit maximization.

Engels observes:

> Among the worst of these towns after Preston and Oldham is Bolton, eleven miles north-west of Manchester. It has, so far as I have been able to observe in my repeated visits, but one main street, a very dirty one, Deansgate, which serves as a market, and is even in the finest weather a dark, unattractive hole in spite of the fact that, except for the factories, its sides are formed by low one and two-storied houses. Here, as everywhere, the older part of the town is especially ruinous and miserable. A dark-coloured body of water, which leaves the beholder in doubt whether it is a brook or a long string of stagnant puddles, flows through the town and contributes its share to the total pollution of the air, by no means pure without it.[21]

It is clear from this passage that Engels was very much aware of the pollution of the air and of the social conditions of the working class. For Marx, there is an even clearer connection between the two. This represents a connection between what he called the "social" and the "environment in our time."

Marx was referring to factory pollution, and thus giving expression to the fact that human beings constitute one of the causal factors of pollution. This is not the only remark that Marx made about environmental damage. In addition to the references to his own time, he also wrote about historical instances of harm to the environment and agriculture. The following passage from Marx illustrates many aspects of environmental degradation throughout history and is worth quoting at length:

> There have been in Asia, generally, from immemorial times, but three departments of Government; that of Finance, or the plunder of the interior; that of War, or the plunder of the exterior; and, finally, the department of Public Works. Climate and territorial conditions, especially the vast tracts of desert, extending from the Sahara, through Arabia, Persia, India, and Tartary, to the most elevated Asiatic highlands, constituted artificial irrigation by canals and water-works the basis of Oriental agriculture. As in Egypt and India, inundations are used for fertilizing the soil in Mesopotamia, Persia, &c.; advantage is taken of a high level for feeding irrigative canals. This prime necessity of an economical and common use of water, which, in the Occident, drove private enterprise to voluntary association, as in Flanders and Italy, necessitated, in the Orient where civilization was too low and the territorial extent too vast to call into life voluntary association, the interference of the centralizing power of Government. Hence an economical function devolved upon all Asiatic Governments, the function of providing public works. This artificial fertilization of the soil, dependent on a Central Government, and immediately decaying with the neglect of irrigation and drainage, explains the otherwise strange fact that we now find whole territories barren and desert that were once brilliantly cultivated, as Palmyra, Petra, the ruins in Yemen, and large provinces of Egypt, Persia, and Hindostan; it also explains how a single war of devastation has been able to depopulate a country for centuries, and to strip it of all its civilization.[22]

Marx explains bad agricultural techniques, water use, and areas that were once fertile but are now desert areas in relation to political and economic developments. What is also remarkable is his indirect acknowledgment that ancient civilizations also acted based on the principle of the conquest of nature. Nature has suffered at the hands of our species. Man's first impulse for self-satisfaction and pleasure demonstrates, in the words of Marx, damage to nature. This was not Marx's only statement on the history of the human impact on nature. In the following passage, he refers to Karl Fraas's study of climate and flora:[23]

> [Fraas] claims that with cultivation—depending on its degree—the 'moisture' so beloved by the peasants gets lost (hence also the plants migrate from south to north), and finally steppe formation occurs. The first effect of cultivation is useful, but finally devastating through deforestation, etc. This man is both a thoroughly learned philologist (he has written books in *Greek*) and a chemist, agronomist, etc. The conclusion is that cultivation—when it proceeds in natural growth and is not *consciously controlled* (as a bourgeois he naturally does not reach this point)—leaves deserts behind it, Persia, Mesopotamia, etc., Greece. So once again an unconscious socialist tendency![24]

Marx explains that deforestation happens when the initially beneficial development of cultivation is left to its own so-called natural growth, without conscious monitoring and control. Such remarks by Marx are especially interesting, since sustainability entails a consciousness that works to lessen significant harm to nature; yet, in the above case, this conclusion, when reached by a bourgeois, evinces an "unconscious socialist tendency."

Several historical examples demonstrating deforestation, water misuse, and damage to the environment appear in Marx. He links these to the underlying economic and political system. This is where the problem of epistemology comes into the picture. Western epistemology has been severely criticized for promoting the dominion of man over nature, which is composed of both organic and inorganic matter. Engels himself seems to be aware of this epistemological problem:

> Let us not, however, flatter ourselves overmuch on account of our human victories over nature. For each such victory nature takes its revenge on us. Each victory, it is true, in the first place brings about the results we expected, but in the second and third places it has quite different, unforeseen effects which only too often cancel the first. The people who, in Mesopotamia, Greece, Asia Minor and elsewhere, destroyed the forests to obtain cultivable land, never dreamed that by removing along with the forests the collecting centres and reservoirs of moisture they were laying the basis for the present forlorn state of those countries.[25]

Another important point is the emphasis on the metabolic interaction between nature and man found in Marx. The concept of metabolic rift, a term coined by John Bellamy Foster,[26] is discussed in the first volume of Marx's *Capital*, in the section on large-scale industry and agriculture in Chapter 15. Here, Marx argues that the intensification of agriculture and the expansion of the capitalist mode of production lead to a disruption of the metabolic relationship between human beings and nature: "Capitalist production, therefore, only develops the techniques and the degree of combination of the social process of production by simultaneously undermining the original sources of all wealth—the soil and the worker."[27] The increase of the population in great centers has two outcomes: it "concentrates the historical motive power of society"[28] and "disturbs the metabolic interaction between man and the earth."[29] Marx refers to this same issue in the third volume of *Capital* when he analyzes the change of population at the expense of agricultural labor and argues that it causes an "irreparable rift in the interdependent process of social metabolism."[30] This allows us to argue that Marx was well aware of the separation of humans from nature brought about by the capitalist mode of production. He was equally aware of the social problems caused by people departing rural locations in search of factory employment in the great urban centers. However, Marx considered these issues in connection with the transition to industrial capitalism.

Engels' reflections on environmental harm, and how unexpected harmful results follow from choices and actions initially believed to be good, find an echo in the Netflix limited series *Unnatural Selection*. This striking series examines whether human-originated technological improvements and genetic modifications might change our individual lives as well as the life of our planet as a whole. In one episode, a young researcher wants to implement a genetic modification on rats that would eliminate the pests for good. However, the project is not welcomed. Indigenous people bluntly stated their objections to the visitor, making clear their discontent, best expressed in the words of one community member:

> You know, we've heard lots and lots of nice words from the colonizers over the millennia, uh, that have to be proven hollow, because underneath it is those hidden agendas. In a sense, historically, you're a little bit like the missionary coming with a good story, but behind you is a whole lot of fellas with some rifles, you know.[31]

Another community member indeed pointed out that the principal financial backer of the project was the Defense Advanced Research Projects Agency

(DARPA), an arms manufacturer. In another case, an Italian proposal to genetically modify only male mosquitoes to help fight malaria in Burkina Faso raised almost identical concerns. Jim Thomas, an environmentalist and advocate, observes that even the best possible research does not warrant the use of results for other malevolent purposes, such as bioweapons.[32] In the two cases, the parties acknowledge the reality of the problem; however, they doubt that artificially induced genetic modification would be able to overcome a natural, biological hazard. When it comes to "acts of God," it is easy to accept catastrophes, but people are much more reluctant to assent to any "unnatural" modification. We should remember that the word "unnatural" signifies a detachment from the natural process. The concept condemns human intervention into natural processes. As they are themselves developed from nature, I do not see human beings as unnatural; this is why I prefer the term "second nature." This can be clarified through another philosophical concept: why are we so ready to accept natural evolution even as we are (or are increasingly becoming) reluctant to accept any human proposal? The reason for this might be the acceptance of or even obedience to supernatural or natural forces in the external world. Yet I would still argue that the opposite might be the case: humans fear humans more than anything else! We could also consider the Covid-19 vaccines. Who would deny that vaccination opponents were those who, to a certain extent, feared the eventual emergence of unexpected side effects? Were they completely wrong? I do not think so. I am vaccinated, but it was a risk I took, calculating the benefit of meeting a present risk greater than potential future harm. In terms of sustainability: how can we know that a technology promoted today as a carbon emission "killer" will not become another hazardous factor in the future?

As we can see, the rise of industrial capitalism, international trade and colonialism, profit maximization, which are specific to industrialization, focuses on productive forces,[33] but not to the benefit of the working class. On the contrary, the suffering of this class increased; they lost their property; and not only did the husbands and fathers of working-class families have to sell their own labor power, but those of their wives and children too. Nevertheless, reading the literature of sustainability makes it possible to see that concerns about climate-related issues were rather acute, and sustainability, ecologism, and environmentalism became systematic after the Second World War.

Post-Second World War: Pioneers of the Ecological Movement

A notable change to the global financial system appears to have been launched by a joint effort by Roosevelt and Churchill in the Second World War. They set up the famous Bretton Woods Conference, which gave birth to the World Bank (WB) and the International Monetary Fund (IMF).

It would not be an exaggeration, at least in capitalist terms, to say that Bretton Woods and its aftermath enabled relatively stable growth in Europe and the USA, as well as in Japan. After the Great Depression of 1929, this new regime had some success in curbing speculative activities by markets; as a result, stock markets depended on real economic outcomes. Nonetheless, the reshaping of the overall banking and finance industries eventually faded. Since the system enjoyed relatively stable growth, pressures for the organization of the banking industry became and then remained dormant. There was success in terms of both economic growth and profitability; as long as the overall system worked, no one troubled the banking and finance industry. Such short- and mid-term vision and politics dismiss the trouble that would inevitably appear at a later stage: deferring trouble is an endemic part of capitalist politics.

As a consequence of its relative success, Bretton Woods was vulnerable to its "killer": financialization. Since the 1970s, we have seen the rapid rise of financialization, stretching into the global economy through the web enabled by US policyholders. Derivatives are the main driver of financialization. Today, it is believed that the overall volume of derivatives exceeds one quadrillion US dollars (or, in other terms, a thousand trillion or a billion billion US dollars). The fragility thus created caused the first collapse of the financial markets in the 2008–2009 crisis, and its impact is still felt in markets and the global economy.

After the end of the Second World War, greenhouse gas emissions increased dramatically,[34] as did the financing of the activities that made them possible. Finance is a method that provides cheap capital to a firm if the applicable interest rate is affordable. With significantly greater debt undertaken to own capital, a firm is able to invest a large amount of money granted by a single bank or a syndicate of banks into a project (e.g., financing a coal mine).

Was the world silent regarding the danger? Or was there any concern or objection raised about these soaring emissions? There was. Two influential texts appeared in roughly the same period. One was Rachel Carson's famous book *Silent Spring*[35] originally published in 1962. Carson was a marine biologist, and her work covers the many ways in which the Earth is harmed by our species. Carson paid special attention to the use of pesticides and warned about the ruin they caused in the environment. The other noteworthy work was by Murray Bookchin, the famous thinker and founder of social ecology, *Our Synthetic Environment* (written under the pseudonym Lewis Herber). Like Carson, Bookchin drew attention to the hazards of synthetic pesticides.

Carson's book quickly gained a significant following, whereas Bookchin's work was largely ignored by the media. Juan Cebada observes that Bookchin's undervalued book had its roots in an article that Bookchin wrote about the harmful impact of chemical substances used in the food industry.[36] He further notes that Bookchin's earlier criticism of experts and the government was justified in light of the hearings of the Committee of the House of Representatives.[37]

So, the first seminal works focused on synthetic chemical substances that harmed the environment, in particular agricultural products and food. In addition, in Carson's work, we see how both our surface and underground water suffer damage. Today it is possible to say that springs are even more silent, despite the myriad of initiatives that claim to fight against climate change, social problems, and the like.

One of Murray Bookchin's most remarkable works was dedicated to ecology and its social aspects. *The Ecology of Freedom*[38] was first published in 1982. It is a seminal work in the field of social ecology, the philosophical and political theory that emphasizes the interconnectedness of social, ecological, and political issues and the need for an integrated approach in addressing them. In *The Ecology of Freedom*, Bookchin advances a critique of hierarchy and dominance, claiming that these forms of social organization are at the source of ecological damage and inequality in society. He also proposes a vision of a decentralized, ecological society based on the principles of direct democracy, mutual aid, and social and ecological interdependence. The book has enjoyed significant influence on environmental and social justice movements around the world.

Bookchin was not the first in the anti-capitalist camp to draw attention to the danger of GHGs. While he is an important figure in the development of social ecology and environmental thought, socialist thinkers raised the dangers of GHGs before the publication of *The Ecology of Freedom*. Earlier, in the 1970s,

Barry Commoner, an American ecologist and socialist, wrote about the risks of GHGs and the need for a radical social and economic transformation to address them. Commoner argued that capitalism and industrialization lay at the root of environmental degradation and climate change, and that a socialist alternative was necessary to ensure a sustainable future.[39] In the 1980s, eco-socialist thinkers like André Gorz[40] and Rudolf Bahro[41] further developed these ideas, emphasizing the need for a decentralized, ecological society that prioritized the needs of people and the planet over profit and economic growth.

As we can see, socialist history did not dismiss the concept of a sustainable planet, although there have been major problems due to the pleasure of tasting power and rude materialistic positivism and determinism. Socialists, including anarchists and critical thinkers, expressed their concern about ecological degradation from different perspectives. They were sometimes harshly critical of each other, but it would not be an exaggeration to say that their main aim was to act against the exploitation of human beings and nature—not separately from each other. The history I presented here is far from adequate or comprehensive. There are a myriad of thinkers and political movements from the so-called "left" that have raised issues about how our planet is being devastated by the exploitation of nature. My goal was to show some breakthroughs, as we live in an era where memories can be reset too quickly. Interestingly, this is not necessarily done by those who are against communal movements; on the contrary, there are too many who claim to be socialists and yet criticize the intellectual side of earlier critical thinkers. Too much self-confidence erases the rigorous thought and action of the past. This unconscious neoliberal inspiration is one of the biggest culprits of critical theory today.

Notes

1 Julie Dahlquist and Rainford Knight, *Principles of Finance* (Houston, TX: OpenStax, 2022), 8; emphasis in original.

2 Frederick Engels, "Preface," in Marx, *Capital*, vol. 3, 91–111.

3 David Harvey, *The Limits to Capital* (London: Verso, 2018), 241.

4 Marx, *Capital*, vol. 1, 184.

5 Ben Fine and Alfredo Saad-Filho, *Marx's Capital*, 5th ed. (London: Pluto Press, 2014), 123.

6 Marx, *Capital*, vol. 3, 728.

7 Ibid.

8 Ibid., 738.

9 Karl Marx, *Theories of Surplus-Value [Volume IV of Capital]* (Moscow: Progress Publishers, 1971), 469; emphasis in original.

10 Ibid.; emphasis in original.

11 Harvey, *The Limits to Capital*, 260.

12 William Leatham. *Letters on the Currency, Addressed to Charles Wood, Esq., M.P., Chairman of the Committee of the House of Commons, Now Sitting; and Ascertaining for the First Time, on True Principles, the Amount of Inland and Foreign Bills of Exchange in Circulation for Several Consecutive Years, and Out at One Time*, 2nd ed. (Cornhill: Pelham Richardson, 1840), 43–4, quoted in Marx, *Capital*, vol. 3, 526.

13 European Commission, "Communication from the Commission. Action Plan: Financing Sustainable Growth," COM(2018) 97 final, Brussels, August 3, 2018, https://eur-lex.europa.eu/legal-content/EN/TXT/?uri=CELEX:52018DC0097.

14 Romain Berrou, Nicola Ciampoli, and Vladimiro Marini, "Defining Green Finance: Existing Standards and Main Challenges," in *The Rise of Green Finance in Europe: Opportunities and Challenges for Issuers, Investors, and Marketplaces*, ed. Marco Migliorelli and Philippe Dessertine (Cham: Palgrave Macmillan, 2019), 31–52.

15 Following the acquisition of Vigeo Eiris.

16 Marx, *Capital*, vol. 3, 612.

17 This measure (rating) may be applied both at the company and transaction levels; it means a company may well have a corporate ESG rating and still have a particular rating for a transaction (say, the issuance of a green bond).

18 Ibid., 956.

19 Henry J. Cadbury, "Another early Quaker Anti-slavery Document," *The Journal of Negro History* 27, no. 2 (1942): 210–15.

20 John Wesley, *The Works of John Wesley, Vol. 6, First Series of Sermons (40–53) Second Series Begun (54–86)* (Albany: Books For The Ages, 1997).

21 Friedrich Engels, *Karl Marx, Frederick Engels: Collected Works, Vol. 4, Marx and Engels: 1844–1845*, 345–6.

22 Karl Marx, *Karl Marx, Frederick Engels: Collected Works, Vol. 12, Marx and Engels: 1853–1854* (London: Lawrence & Wishart, 1975), 127.

23 Karl N. Fraas, *Climate and Plant Life in der Zeit, ein Beitrag zur Geschichte beider* (Landshut: J. G. Wölfe, 1847).

24 Friedrich Engels, *Karl Marx, Frederick Engels: Collected Works, Vol. 42, Marx and Engels: 1864–1868*, 559; emphasis in original.

25 Friedrich Engels, *Karl Marx, Frederick Engels: Collected Works, Vol. 25, Engels*, 460–1.
26 John Bellamy Foster, *Marx's Ecology: Materialism and Nature* (New York: Monthly Review Press, 2000), ix.
27 Marx, *Capital*, vol. 1, 638.
28 Ibid., 637.
29 Ibid.
30 Marx, *Capital*, vol. 3, 949.
31 "Changing an Entire Species," the third episode in the first season of the Netflix series *Unnatural Selection*.
32 Ibid.
33 Ellen Meiksins Wood, *The Origin of Capitalism: A Longer View* (London: Verso, 2017). I would recommend the whole book to the reader since it describes in detail how the transition to industrial capitalism occurred in the United Kingdom rather than in France, Florence, or the Dutch Kingdom.
34 See Bruno Venditti, "Here's how CO2 Emissions have Changed since 1900," *World Economic Forum*, November 22, 2022, https://www.weforum.org/agenda/2022/11/visualizing-changes-carbon-dioxide-emissions-since-1900/.
35 Rachel Carson, *Silent Spring* (Boston: Mariner Books, 2002). This is considered the seminal work that launched the ecological movement.
36 Juan Diego Perez Cebada, "An Editorial Flop Revisited: Rethinking the impact of Murray Bookchin's *Our Synthetic Environment* on its Golden *Anniversary," Global Environment: A Journal of Transdisciplinary History* 6, no. 12 (2013): 250–73. See Lewis Herber, "The Problem of Chemicals in Food," *Contemporary Issues: A Magazine for a Democracy of Content* 3, no. 12 (1952): 206–41.
37 Cebada, "An Editorial Flop," 252.
38 Murray Bookchin, *The Ecology of Freedom: The Emergence and Dissolution of Hierarchy* (Montreal: Black Rose Books).
39 Barry Commoner, *The Closing Circle: Nature, Man, and Technology* (New York: Alfred A. Knopf, 1971).
40 André Gorz, *Ecology as Politics*, trans. Patsy Vigderman and Jonathan Cloud (Boston: South End Press, 1980).
41 Rudolf Bahro, *From Red to Green*, trans. Gus Fagan and Richard Hurst (London: Verso, 1984).

3

Sustainable Finance

Mainstream Concepts and Events

In this chapter, we will visit how the ruling system of power perceives sustainability concerns and warnings, and what initiatives and actions it takes. I will start with a well-known concept of sustainability, Corporate Social Responsibility (CSR), with the aim of unveiling it. Sustainability reporting is the main paradigm in the corporate sector, and publishing sustainability reports is now a must rather than an option. I will then introduce two major initiatives that I consider to be the backbone of decarbonization scenarios and pathways: the Intergovernmental Panel on Climate Change (IPCC) and the International Energy Agency (IEA). Citation and explanation of historical breakthroughs will follow. All these mainstream facts will form a further basis for the critical review of sustainability and Sustainable Finance.

Subsection A: Mainstream Concepts and Paradigms

Corporate Social Responsibility (CSR)[1]

It would be an exaggeration to claim that industrial capital ignored environmental and social issues. The important point to keep in mind is that a black-and-white approach is insufficient; rather, we need to realize that capitalism has immanent elements that lie beyond good and evil. Certainly, there are many people and firms that care about the environment and social issues. However, the laws of motion of capitalism would lead to the same results sooner or later. The problem does not lie within the boundaries of a moral framework. The system itself requires certain rules that cannot be encompassed by purely ethical propositions and approaches; the problems exceed the boundaries of ethics.

Until the twentieth century, CSR was based on philanthropy. Over time, more determinate responsibilities evolved. John Elkington, a business writer, coined the term "triple bottom line" (TBL).[2] The three bottom lines encompassed are the social, environmental, and economics systems supposed to be governed properly. In time, TBL gave way to "sustainability," and Elkington admitted that his term became obsolete. Now the main term in use is "sustainability"; however, ESG is also used interchangeably with sustainability.

Another decades-old term is "Corporate Social Responsibility." As the term itself suggests, CSR represents the socially responsible acts of a corporation. Specific to the social aspect of their activity, CSR represents the ethical responsibilities of businesses aiming to align with their stakeholders regarding behaviors and values. Stakeholders are of various kinds and differ from shareholders. Stakeholders include customers, supply chain firms, interest groups, employees, and others.[3] To take a simple but illustrative example, a firm should not operate in an environment that endangers the lives of a neighboring community. CSR, in accordance with its concept, includes charity and corporate assistance for local communities, and more broadly, for society. However, charity and philanthropy are not the same as CSR. A business may be philanthropic but suffer from poor governance. This was the case with Parmalat in Italy when it was filed for bankruptcy in 2003 due to a scandal.[4] This indicates that an ethical code is one-half of the game; the other is governance.

Carson and Bookchin, along with other ecologists, recorded the harm being done to the planet, but sustainability and social responsibility in businesses relate to another concept: profitability. That is, ecologists and social thinkers are driven to transform the planet and society; businesses endeavor to find paths to maximize value for their stakeholders while focusing on financial targets and shareholder values. The attempt to synthesize shareholder profitability and value to shareholders, and society in general, is the main driver for capital, with or without ecological or social considerations. If reconciliation between profitability and eco-social considerations is not accomplished, firms run the risk of ensuring their own (profit-oriented) sustainability. The idea is to achieve maximum profitability while acting in line with the values of stakeholders. Would it ever be truly possible to maximize profits while respecting the values of stakeholders and meeting environmental and social responsibilities? One of the goals of this study is to provide an answer to this question.

CSR reflects the ethical approach of the owners of capital. A good example would be the case of the Economy of Communion (EoC) enterprises initiated in Brazil in 1991 by Chiara Lubich. Lubich witnessed social inequality and poverty.[5] Maria-Gabriella Baldarelli, Mara Del Baldo, and Caterina Ferrone provide empirical analyses of two companies that act as samples from Italy. The first is Ridix S.p.A, a company founded in 1969 in Grugliasco in Turin. The second is Arcobaleno in Valdarno SRL (limited company), founded in 2006. In their concluding remarks, the authors observe that participation in corporate governance constitutes "a true relationship character"[6] focused on trust. These EoC companies, they maintain, strive to serve the community based on its needs, and their operations are founded on the conception of human dignity. Moreover, these sublime ambitions emerge from the "charisma" radiated by the initial founder, Lubich.

Reading the article leads us to the conclusion that social responsibility is the fruit of charisma! The charisma of the initial aspirant spreads from this source and endows its charm first to companies and then to the community. The article contains some passages noting, for example, that Arcobaleno in Valdarno behaves responsibly, like a law-abiding person. If two employees steal, they will not necessarily be treated in the same way; an investigation will be carried out. Maybe one of them will regret and repent, while the other remains adamant.[7] Such theatrical descriptions aim to convince us of the transformation both companies underwent, and yet they are extraordinary examples of service to the community.

I was curious and looked at the websites of both companies. The first is a small company that produces machinery, with a social capital of a little more than half a million euros, which claims that its production stage is environmentally friendly. No publicly available financial statements, no sustainability reports; simply statements and a small enterprise serving the charismatic founder's main purpose. However, I could find nothing about the other company; their website,[8] launched by the charismatic and charming founder, did not giving any information. Instead, a page in Chinese shows up, and based on the appearance of the website, it looked like I had made some money! I cannot know for sure, but it may be that the company has since departed the business world despite all its charismatic engagements. I stress the word "charisma" and its derivatives; they work to hide the nature of finance. Chiara Lubich could indeed be an individual with high ethical values, genuinely wanting a society where poverty does not exist. However, one of the main suppositions of this study is that, regardless of personal ambition, no effort will bring salvation to the masses if the ownership of the productive forces remains in the hands of a minority.

CSR was tested during Covid-19. A concept that has been around for decades was put to the test by the pandemic. Research shows that while some companies responded quickly to the catastrophic events caused by the virus, many others did not. On the positive side, attention to hygienic delivery of goods, adapting and organizing workplaces to make them healthier and safer, and promoting remote working to protect employees as stakeholders were notable. On the negative side, to keep sales active, many workers had to work overtime, putting themselves at risk. Companies struggling to maintain profitability were more concerned with survival than with CSR. Therefore, companies that have resources and are pioneers in their industries have, in a sense, shown that they can contribute to the fight against such catastrophic events. Nevertheless, it is what has emerged, and it applies to pioneering companies. Archie B. Carroll states that CSR during Covid-19 was a test that forced companies to rethink and reconsider CSR. She also believes that because of the pioneering companies, the others would also apply better CSR toward their stakeholders.[9]

When we look at the interpretations of CSR during Covid-19, we see that some companies only appeared to be socially responsible and green. In fact, they were not much different from those who did not promote CSR. On the other hand, if we go deeper in our understanding and analysis, CSR reflects hegemony. The big and strong apply it at a certain level and the others are expected to follow. This is where the dialectical logic realizes that such companies—small and medium enterprises—cannot always follow the big ones due to scarcity, lack of human resources, and profitability of the former. Here, apart from the big names such as Amazon and Google, small and medium-sized companies really suffered during the pandemic. For them, preparing and publishing sustainability or CSR reports, allocating funds and resources is a luxury; they are trying to survive because the pandemic has hit not only the working class in society but also businesses. Therefore, CSR in its essence represents inequality in a hidden form, while promoting ethics and care for others. It is intrinsic to the structure of the existing society and mode of production that some companies can adopt it while many others cannot. Beyond the rhetoric lies the cold truth: CSR is promoted by giants, and others are forced to follow. Those who cannot follow—which will be the inevitable case—will go out of business; this is the hidden hegemonic structure. Now we can understand why CSR communication reflects the real operations of some companies, while it is just talk for many others. It is not their individual fault; it is a fault related to the structure of the current economic system. This also shows us, based on the analysis of society and the economic system, that ethical considerations are the result of the surrounding production modes. For a truly ethical society, it is essential to evaluate the modes of production and their ownership.

Dialectical reasoning, when applied, unveils what lies beyond the appearing virtue and responsibilities of corporations. Both capital and corporate social responsibility are represented as components of a firm; capital is required for the operations—for example, production—of the firm, and CSR for the social aspects. Implicit here are the details of the determinants of these responsibilities. In its current version, defined and presented as the evolution of philanthropy, a firm's social responsibility is represented as the outcome of an immanent historical development. However, such representation fully hides social inequalities caused by capital itself, that is, the very nature of capital and the struggle between the owners of capital and the working class. In fact, CSR is not a favor bestowed by a firm on communities, but a historically gained achievement won by the resistance of external forces and imposed on companies. We can be confident that almost no firm would adopt CSR without resistance from external parties.

Two Major Initiatives: The IPCC AR6 and the IEA Net Zero Emissions (NZE) 2050

When it comes to climate scenarios and pathways, it is a must for financial institutions to refer to the two main organizations: the IPCC and the IEA. Both organizations have recognized climate scenarios for net zero carbon dioxide by 2050. Today, it is a must for most financial institutions to set their climate or financed emissions targets based on the 6th Assessment Report of the IPCC and the net zero scenario of the IEA (IEA NZE 2050). Both bodies publish their reports at intervals and provide projections about mid- and long-term possible paths regarding where the planet may evolve amid different scenarios. Although criticized by some climate experts and activists, I still see both organizations as major components of climate science as they both inform us of the possible outcomes based on facts. The important point is that both provide us with extensive information about climate change and how this would inform our future projections.

The IPCC AR6

The IPCC stands for "The Intergovernmental Panel on Climate Change." We learn from their website that it was founded in 1988 by the United Nations Environment Programme (UNEP) and the World Meteorological Organization (WMO) and endorsed by the United Nations General Assembly in the same year.[10] The goal of the IPCC has been since then to present the state of climate change and explore its economic and social impacts.

The IPCC provides Assessment Reports (ARs). The latest AR is AR6, which was initiated for the cycle from 2015 to 2023. The IPCC AR6 is the product of this cycle, and it consisted of three Working Group Reports that were the product of intensive research that amounted to more than 6,000 pages!

It is not possible to cite a detailed summary of the AR6 in this book, but we will take a look at what makes it so important in terms of Sustainable Finance. We should then first grasp what the relation of the AR to the finance field is. As mentioned, there have been three reports under the AR6. The first one was from Working Group I (WG I): "Climate Change 2021: The Physical Science Basis."[11] In this report, the WG elaborated the then state of the climate. The main findings of the report emphasized that humans caused global warming more than other factors. In other words, anthropogenic factors played a significant part in the warming of the planet. These adverse effects increased compared to the previous AR (AR5), according to the report. The key point in the report is that CO_2 and GHG emissions must drop significantly in the next decades to avoid global warming as well as to limit it up to 1.5°C and 2°C compared to preindustrial levels. As we can see, the AR6 also discussed possible futures under different scenarios after the presentation of the then current state. And as we can see, the future is not bright at all unless significant GHG emissions decrease in the near future.

The second part of the AR6 was the report of the WG II: "Climate Change 2022: Impacts, Adaptation and Vulnerability."[12] In this report, we can see the possible detrimental effects of climate change. For instance, AR6 recognizes the differentiated impacts of climate change among different regions and socioeconomic structures. It means more forced migration, poverty, and collapse, unless solutions are provided.

The third part of the AR6 was "Climate Change 2022: Mitigation of Climate Change" by WG III. This report explored the sources of GHG emissions and cited developments made for reducing such emissions and mitigating relevant risks. It also discussed national pledges provided by countries and their possible impact on reducing emissions.

For our purposes, although the whole report is crucial as well as the Synthesis Report published in March 2023, what is important to keep in mind is that unless there is a very strong rationale for doing otherwise, financial institutions should align themselves with the IPCC AR6 scenarios that limit global warming to 1.5°C. Of course, this is not a clear-cut scenario. First, scenarios have probabilities because they are based on statistical information. For example, if we talk about a 50 percent probability of 1.5°C warming, then the carbon budget of the scenarios is 500 Gt (gigatons) and 400 Gt if we want a 67 percent probability. We will discuss more about that in the discussion of financed emissions and financed emissions targets. Second, some scenarios do not incur overshooting, which means temperature rise goes above 1.5°C for some decades and then goes under this value. And some scenarios either have limited overshooting (temporary) or no overshooting at all. These types of scenarios are classified as C1 category scenarios that limit the warming to 1.5°C with low or no overshooting. And these are the scenarios that must be used by financial institutions for setting financed emissions (with a 50 percent probability in general). Therefore, it is logical to say that financial institutions are requested to use the strictest scenarios. It also means that they face or will face issues if the real economy continues its activities on a "business-as-usual" basis. The IPCC (and IEA as well) present the differences between these scenarios and both show how 1.5°C scenarios call for immediate action.

IPCC AR6 scenarios, on the other hand, are not directly useful for financial institutions. Although it is the backbone of the transition policies, deriving sectoral pathways from it is not an easy task—if not impossible at all. This is why financial institutions generally tend to build their climate targets based on the IEA NZE 2050 scenario and relevant pathways.

The IEA NZE 2050

The IEA stands for "The International Energy Agency." Its establishment was earlier than the IPCC. Following the disruption in the oil industry and the collapse of Bretton Woods, 1974 was the establishment year of the IEA's establishment. As a side note, we see another example of how nothing actually comes out of the blue. This is the strongest part of the materialist conception of history. When we look back in history, we would hardly find any event or initiative free of relations to social or economic situations in the world. The history of finance, in that respect too, justifies these relational or causal facts on much more solid ground compared to anti-dialectical tools and paths.

Speaking of the IEA, what is important for us in particular is the IEA NZE 2050. The Net Zero Emissions by 2050 Scenario (NZE Scenario) presents a roadmap for the global energy sector to achieve net zero CO_2 emissions by 2050, with advanced economies reaching this goal sooner than others.[13] This scenario aligns with key energy-related Sustainable Development Goals (SDGs), such as universal access to energy by 2030 and significant improvements in air quality. It is consistent with limiting global temperature rise to 1.5°C, with at least a 50 percent chance of success, in line with the emissions reductions outlined in the Intergovernmental Panel on Climate Change (IPCC)'s Sixth Assessment Report. As we mentioned in the IPCC section above, IPCC AR6 is the backbone of all relevant scenarios. Nonetheless, the IEA NZE 2050 draws its own scenario based on a 50 percent probability, which is a fair probability. Remember, a 67 percent probability decreases the carbon budget from 500 to 400 Gt CO_2—to realize how probabilities can affect the outcomes.

Following the 2021 NZE Scenario[14] and in line with it, the 2023 NZE update describes a pathway for the global energy sector to reach net zero CO_2 emissions by 2050 by deploying a wide range of clean energy technologies. Decisions about which technologies to deploy are guided by factors such as costs, technological maturity, market conditions, existing infrastructure, and policy preferences. The scenario prioritizes a smooth transition to ensure energy security through coordinated policies and incentives, allowing all stakeholders to anticipate the rapid changes required and to minimize energy market volatility and the risk of stranded assets. The rapid deployment of clean energy technologies and improvements in energy efficiency are at the core of this transition. The scenario is based on a detailed analysis of the lead times required for mineral supplies and clean energy technologies to ensure the feasibility of this transition.

The NZE Scenario represents one possible path, rather than the only path to net zero emissions. In recent years, the energy sector has been responsible for about three-quarters of global greenhouse gas emissions. Achieving net zero energy-related CO_2 emissions by 2050 would require ambitious and immediate actions. The scenario also considers CO_2 reductions from land use that would align with the energy sector transformation, working in collaboration with the International Institute for Applied Systems Analysis (IIASA).

In addition to the IEA NZE 2050 scenario, the IEA also provides the World Energy Outlook (WEO) every year based on evidence and provides large datasets about industries, among which is an emissions factor database that unfortunately requires a purchase.

The IEA NZE 2050 draws its scenarios and pathways upon renewable energy and technologies such as carbon capture, utilization, and storage (CCUS). Additionally, achieving net zero CO_2 emissions in the energy sector by 2050 depends on fair and effective global cooperation. The pathway to net zero emissions by 2050 is very narrow, requiring all countries to contribute to achieving this goal, provided that advanced economies take the lead and reach net zero emissions earlier than emerging markets and developing economies, as mentioned. The scenario envisions achieving global access to electricity and clean cooking by 2030, in line with established SDGs. Considering other greenhouse gases, rapid and significant reductions in methane emissions from the oil, gas, and coal sectors are considered to be time buyers for less abrupt CO_2 reductions in emerging markets and developing economies. Global collaboration is essential to develop and implement ambitious policies, reduce the costs of clean technologies, and scale up diverse and resilient global supply chains for critical minerals and clean energy technologies. Enhanced financial support to emerging markets and developing economies is a critical component of this collaborative effort.

Other Net Zero Scenarios

There are several other net zero models provided by different institutes. Among them is the Network for Greening the Financial System (NGFS), which is worth mentioning. The NGFS, founded in 2017, is an initiative of central banks, academics, and supervisors that aims to accelerate the transition to green finance. Among its aims, providing scenarios and relevant recommendations to central banks plays a crucial role. NGFS scenarios are especially useful for grasping the models and scenarios used for Sustainable Finance. The Network for Greening the Financial System (NGFS) uses a variety of Integrated Assessment Models (IAMs) in the development of its climate scenarios. These models are complex computer simulations that integrate knowledge from different disciplines, such as economics, energy systems, and climate science, to project future climate and socioeconomic trajectories. Three prominent IAMs used by the NGFS are REMIND-MAgPIE, MESSAGEix-GLOBIOM, and GCAM.

REMIND-MAgPIE, developed by the Potsdam Institute for Climate Impact Research, focuses on technology-rich representations of energy and land use systems. It is characterized by its exploration of the role of different technologies and policies in the mitigation of climate change.

MESSAGEix-GLOBIOM combines a detailed representation of the energy system with a focus on land use dynamics, developed by the International Institute for Applied Systems Analysis (IIASA). It is particularly useful for analyzing the interactions between energy production, agriculture, and forestry.

GCAM, developed by the Joint Global Change Research Institute, is a global model that represents the economy as a whole, including the energy system, the land use system, the water system, and the climate system. It is well suited for analyzing the broader economic impacts of climate change and climate policy.

These models differ in their specific focus and methodology, although they share the common goal of assessing climate change and its impacts. REMIND-MAgPIE emphasizes technological solutions, MESSAGEix-GLOBIOM emphasizes land use changes, and GCAM provides a comprehensive economic perspective. These differences lead to differences in their projections, in particular with respect to the feasibility and the costs of different pathways to mitigate climate change. The NGFS takes account of these differences and uses the models in a complementary manner, building on their strengths to provide a more comprehensive understanding of the risks and opportunities associated with climate change for the financial sector.

Following the major concepts about sustainability and climate scenarios in their relationship with the financial system, we can now discuss important mainstream events related to these concepts.

Subsection B: Important Events

From Rio to UN SDGs and the Paris Agreement (1992–2015)

Following the above definition of Sustainable Finance and its emergence as a concept arising from ethical considerations, and citing the thinkers from the socialist camp who drew attention to environmental and ecological hazards, I will now turn to principal mainstream historical events.

A satisfactory presentation of historical facts regarding Sustainable Finance can be found at the website of the United Nations Environment Programme Finance Initiative (UNEP FI), providing information from 1992—the year of its inauguration—to 2022.[15] There we learn that so-called "visionary leaders" had the idea of transforming finance. Here again, we see another charming word: "visionary." Charismatic, visionary: these are the characteristics of the leaders and their guidance, aspirations, and powers of innovation—as though no one had thought about these problems before, and no one had cautioned about the ecological issues that threaten our planet and our lives. I have already provided some examples of other thinkers and environmentalists for whom ecological and social issues were already a matter of concern. Of course, these visionary leaders were not thinkers, or activists with an academic background, or anything of the like; instead, they were the proponents of finance capital. This is one of the most prominent features of capitalism: to give the impression that any initiative, whatever the subject matter, is always its own production. One would not deny that capitalism succeeds in this.

From Rio to Kyoto

Following the UNEP FI, the United Nations Framework Convention on Climate Change (UNFCCC), an international environmental treaty, came into force in March 1994, following its adoption at the Rio Summit of 1992. The target was to "stabilize greenhouse gas concentrations in the atmosphere at a level that would prevent dangerous anthropogenetic interference with the climate system."[16] The key words here, which have appeared especially over the last two decades, are "greenhouse gas emissions" and derivatives of "anthropos," including the Anthropocene, which we will discuss in detail later. It should be kept in mind that since the time this statement was made, environmental concerns have been based on GHGs, and the culprit has been "anthropos": human beings. As another outcome of the UNFCCC launch, the first annual meeting of the UNEP FI was held in Switzerland in September 1994. The topic was "Greening Financial Markets." Greening financial markets: the meaning is that financial markets were financing "brown" investments but were going to initiate "green" financing that would help corporations and governments transform their operations to achieve a green and sustainable planet. Once again, capitalism disguises everything old in the modern dress of a new paradigm.

From Kyoto to Paris with Millennium Development Goals (MDGs)

In December 1997, the well-known Kyoto Protocol was adopted at the conference hosted by the UNFCCC. The parties to the protocol committed themselves to achieving emission reduction targets. It was a binding commitment. A binding set of GHG reduction targets was finally achieved. Finally achieved, but then there arises the question: what was accomplished in concrete terms? Now that we have the possibility to go back and scrutinize the history of Sustainable Finance, this question assumes a degree of urgency because there followed another "binding," and much more sensational agreement in 2015 (The Paris Agreement). This means that the proponents of capital not only launch a paradigm but close a chapter at will. When and if they see it as to their own benefit, they simply exercise their privilege to launch anew.

Fifteen years after its adoption, Colin Hunt noted that the Kyoto Protocol was "doomed . . . because it did not encompass the world's largest and fastest growing economies; it excluded developing countries (including the Peoples [*sic*] Republic of China) from binding targets, and the USA failed to sign up."[17] On the basis of these details, it could be argued that the protocol would have been successful and GHG emissions reduction targets met at the global level if the agreement were broader in scope and included almost all countries. This is a very straightforward assumption, but one that relies on the commitment of individual states. However, this and other similar arguments fail to address the basic reason. The question should be: If all countries were to sign and commit to GHG emission reductions, would success be assured? Those advancing the arguments would answer affirmatively, apparently. My answer, on the contrary, would be "no." The problem does not lie in the quantitative aspect—the number of participants—but in qualitative details: who are the signatories and what do they represent? We will cover this discussion further through the interpretation of the 2015 Paris Agreement.

When the Kyoto Protocol was in force, despite its shortcomings, eight MDGs, prototypes of the Sustainable Development Goals (SDGs), were ratified at the Millennium Summit. The UN Millennium Declaration aimed at the reduction of extreme poverty—its social aspect—and set out eight specific targets to be reached by 2015. These eight goals were:

- Eradicate extreme poverty and hunger.
- Achieve universal primary education.
- Promote gender equality and empower women.
- Reduce child mortality.
- Improve maternal health.
- Combat HIV/AIDS and other diseases.
- Ensure environmental sustainability.
- Develop a global partnership for development.

All were concerned with social problems.

Figure 3.1 depicts these MDGs.

The goals were not reached by 2015. Nonetheless, we cannot deny that there was some success. There was an increase in female members of parliament, extreme poverty declined, primary education rates increased, maternal health improved; however, gender inequality persisted, social and economic inequalities were still significant, and conflicts posed a major threat.[18] What was entirely missing in the MDGs was any consideration of human rights. MDGs would later be superseded by "Sustainable Development Goals."

Both the Kyoto Protocol and the contemporaneous MDGs were unsuccessful to a significant extent, regardless of the motivation of the participants and those charged with meeting the goals. Explanations—or, rather, excuses—listed insufficient staff, organization, collaboration, and the like. In fact, the

Figure 3.1 United Nations Millennium Development Goals (MDGs).

hidden truth is that such initiatives again failed to reflect the apparent truth: those to blame for the issues were supposed to solve them.

While both the Kyoto Protocol and the MDGs were in force, in August 2002, the UNEP FI published, for the first time, a major report on climate change. The *CEO Briefing on Climate Change* demonstrated the relevance of climate change to the financial services industry.[19] It was the first published attempt to invite the financial services industry into the climate change framework. The purpose was to gain the industry's participation in the field within long-term and market-based frameworks. This undertaking was followed by the Equator Principles in June 2003. These principles concerned environmental and social risks in project finance. Minimum standards of due diligence were to be put in place to support responsible risk decision-making. In the area of finance, UNEP FI highlighted its achievements, such as raising financial institutions' awareness of climate change, at Conference of the Parties (COP)9.

As we can see from these historical facts, finance, no matter its color (green, brown, or other), is an integral part of the world system and the world economy. First, the framework is designed, and then financiers are invited to supply the means to realize development goals. This is one of the peculiarities of the financial system: no company, not even a government, would invest without the participation of financing partners or vehicles. There have been several other initiatives designed to integrate the financial industry.

In December 2005, at COP11, the UNEP FI Climate Change Working Group (CCWG) called for assurances to spur much-needed medium- and long-term investment in the transition to a low-carbon economy. The Principles for Responsible Investment (PRI) were launched in April 2006. With nearly 1,500 signatories from more than fifty countries representing US$60 trillion, the PRI has become the reference point for institutional investors committed to responsible, long-term action to integrate environmental, social, and governance issues into investment practices. October 2006 saw the publication of the famous *Stern Review on the Economics of Climate Change*. According to this report, addressing climate change is a pro-growth strategy in the long term and can benefit both rich and poor countries. In July 2012, the report *Lenses and Clocks: Financial Stability and Systemic Risks* was published. This document highlights the importance of gaining a better understanding of broader systemic risk problems, improved governance, and clear fiduciary duties. In July 2015, the United Nations Environment Programme (UNEP), through Redesigning

Finance for Sustainable Development, an event at the Third International Conference on Financing for Development in Addis Ababa, "called for a 'loud revolution' to mobilise the trillions of dollars needed for the transition to a greener, more sustainable world economy."[20] In October 2015, following the announcement of the Sustainable Development Goals, which will be presented in our next section, a group of banks and investors released the Positive Impact Manifesto, calling for a new financing paradigm. According to the manifesto, a new impact-based approach founded on a holistic consideration of the three pillars of sustainable development was needed to overcome the financing gap for sustainable development and achieve the SDGs.

Taking place just before the adoption of the UN SDGs and the Paris Agreement in 2015, the above-mentioned initiatives, with the exception of the Positive Impact Manifesto that followed the announcement of the SDGs, indicate that the financial system should enter the world of sustainability as an indispensable partner. It must be noted that the financial industry's own aspiration in entering the industry was to ensure the profitability of financial institutions in the long run. The emphasis on profitability is essential to win over financial institutions; without it, they would prefer to fund other sectors rather than become saints.

United Nations SDGs and the Paris Agreement in 2015

In January 2015, the General Assembly of the UN began negotiations to reach a post-MDG consensus. The outcome was the adoption of the 2030 Agenda for Sustainable Development. Seventeen SDGs constituted the main part of this agenda, accepted at the UN Sustainable Development Summit in September 2015.

Three months after the adoption of the SDGs, the well-known Paris Agreement was signed in December 2015. One hundred and ninety-five nations agreed to fight climate change by, among other things, undertaking actions and investments for low carbon emissions and a sustainable future. The most important part of the Paris Agreement was the commitment to keep the twenty-first-century global temperature rise well below 2°C (revised to 1.5°C above preindustrial levels).

Currently, along with subsequent initiatives and regulations, the SDGs and the Paris Agreement still constitute the paradigm of Sustainability and are related to Sustainable Finance, which aligns with them in several respects. UNEP FI, Principles of Responsible Banking (PRB), and many other initiatives are linked to both the UN SDGs and the Paris Agreement. The SDGs are intended to be reached by 2030, whereas the Paris Agreement calls for significant reductions in greenhouse gas emissions by 2030 and a net zero carbon world by 2050.

Later initiatives, principles, and finance industry regulations are linked to SDGs and/or the Paris Agreement. For example, in January 2017, nearly two dozen prominent global banks and investors with combined assets of several trillion dollars launched the UNEP FI Principles for Positive Impact Finance with the goal of contributing to the achievement of the SDGs. The principles required a holistic appraisal of positive and negative impacts on economic development, human well-being, and the environment. In November 2018, the "Rethinking Impact to Finance the SDGs" report was published. This report explores innovative approaches to substantially decrease the cost of achieving the SDGs while encouraging business and financing solutions. Social, economic, and environmental impacts have "an as yet under-explored potential to generate financial revenues."[21] We see how necessary it is that the motivation for financing contains a reference to revenues. Green finance does not change this basic fact.

On September 22 and 23, 2019, the Principles for Responsible Banking were launched at the United Nations Annual General Assembly in New York. These principles, led by 130 banks managing tens of trillions of assets, align banks with the societal goals outlined in the SDGs and the Paris Climate Agreement. Since 2015 and the adoption of the UN SDGs and the Paris Agreement, it is clear that the financial industry has become increasingly engaged in Sustainable Finance. This should not be surprising given the temperature reduction targets and the role of finance in Article 2 of the Paris Agreement:

Article 2.

1. This Agreement, in enhancing the implementation of the Convention, including its objective, aims to strengthen the global response to the threat of climate change, in the context of sustainable development and efforts to eradicate poverty, including by:

(a) Holding the increase in the global average temperature to well below 2°C above preindustrial levels and pursuing efforts to limit the temperature increase to 1.5°C above preindustrial levels, recognizing that this would significantly reduce the risks and impacts of climate change;

(b) Increasing the ability to adapt to the adverse impacts of climate change and foster climate resilience and low greenhouse gas emissions development in a manner that does not threaten food production; and

(c) Making finance flows consistent with a pathway toward low greenhouse gas emissions and climate-resilient development.[22]

Historical analysis compels us to determine the causes of this drive. Why did the initiative fail or underperform prior to 2015, and why did it gain greater acceptance after the SDGs and the Paris Agreement? Is it the case that climate awareness finally took root? Or did other motives play a role in driving financial institutions to take part in this sector? It is important to remember that the Paris Agreement envisaged that global temperature should not rise beyond 1.5°C above preindustrial levels. This requires finance flows to align with the implementation of lower greenhouse gas emissions targets. The Paris Agreement clearly links the role of finance to the success of meeting these targets. This historical statement enables us to observe that financial capital is inseparable from the paradigm of climate change. This integration—obligatory for imposing climate change under the dominion of corporations, states, and their apparatuses—makes it clear that changes and/or failures will depend on the involvement of financial capital, a party to the capitalist camp that claims to be fighting against climate change.

Review of COP26, COP27, and COP28 under Sustainable Finance

Up to this point, I have reviewed significant historical events in the development of Sustainable Finance. More recent important occurrences—and in such an ultra-dynamic field these take place almost every day—would help us understand the present state of the process. The expectation, based on the integrity of our analysis, is that these new events would be in line with the earlier ones. As stated earlier, Sustainable Finance must explain itself through its own process. If we can isolate and capture the features of this evolving process, then our analysis would demonstrate internal consistency. With that said, let's look at the two major recent events related to Climate Change: COP26 and COP27.

COP26 in Glasgow

COP26 was another in a series of UN climate summits that provoked great expectations and ended with disappointment. The BBC summarized the agreement, which consists of four main points: emissions, coal, developing countries, and fossil fuel subsidies.[23] Although the agreement was not legally binding, the parties agreed—eventually with reference to COP27—to further reduce carbon emissions, since GHGs are the principal cause of global warming. There was strong pressure to meet the aforementioned 1.5°C target. Of course, the phrase "well below 2°C," used in the Paris Agreement, is rather vague. The world has already suffered significant impacts, increasing temperatures by about 1.2°C above preindustrial levels. How would limiting the increase to less than 2°C help prevent further damage?

The parties agreed on a commitment to "phase down" the use of coal. They could not agree on a "phase out" resolution. The BBC reported that the intervention of India and China forced this compromise.[24] A fund has been pledged to assist developing countries in their efforts to combat the harmful effects of climate change. The fund is estimated at US$1 trillion a year starting in 2025; however, it should be noted that rich countries failed to provide even US$100 billion in 2020.[25] One firm-seeming statement promised to phase out government subsidies that lowered the price of oil, gas, and coal. Yet no start date was determined.

One additional agreement directly involved financial institutions. Financial institutions that controlled US$130 trillion agreed to back clean energy initiatives, such as renewables. They would also divest from industries with significant involvement in fossil fuels. This certainly looked promising. Below, I will further discuss the steps taken by some European banks. As I will demonstrate, some banks indeed have robust policies regarding fossil fuel burning sectors. Nonetheless, following COP26, they were criticized for caring more about public relations (PR) and for not having a sufficiently firm commitment. The result was that, despite some achievements, most bank pledges were still based on self-monitoring. The historical record shows that this is not enough.

COP27 in Sharm el-Sheikh, Egypt

COP27 is presented as a breakthrough by some officials and proponents of the UN Climate Change initiative. They base this on the agreement to establish a "loss and damage" fund, promoted as a key victory in the long struggle to assure help to poor communities.[26] The purpose of the fund is to assist endangered countries by covering the costs incurred from damage caused by global warming and rising sea levels. The establishment of such a fund had been under discussion since the 2013 Warsaw COP. The then chief negotiator for the Philippines, now the Head of Greenpeace South Asia, Yeb Sano, called the 2022 approval of the fund a "new dawn for climate justice."[27] The breakthrough that enabled the establishment of the "loss and damage fund" was apparently a change of attitude on the part of the United States, which had initially opposed the fund. In the years to come, we will see how the fund develops. The current understanding is that an interim committee of twenty-four national representatives would decide how the Fund, and its contributors, would operate. The current understanding is that an interim board of twenty-four national representatives would decide how the Fund, and its contributors, would operate. The committee will share its findings and recommendations at COP28.

Alok Sharma, the British politician who presided over COP26 in Glasgow, was rather critical of the outcome of the summit. Like other campaigners and governments, he was critical of the fossil fuel commitments. For Sharma, the essential 1.5°C target "remains on life support."[28] Commitments and pledges will not achieve much if they are not truly—legally—binding, and not left to the mercy of self-monitoring corporations and organizations. Unless such a definitive measure is taken, reducing carbon emissions caused by oil and gas, and fossil fuels in general, will not be possible.

Great Britain, together with some other governments, including the EU, wanted to reach a binding agreement to ensure that peak emissions would be reached no later than 2025. To achieve this, a clear path for the phasing out of coal and other fossil fuels needed to be determined. These demands were not honored, and they were not part of the agreement text. As a result, the COP26 coal phase-out target was not met; the situation is worse with respect to the target for all other fossil fuels.

Perhaps the most catastrophic failure of COP27 was the lack of a consensus on the 1.5°C target deemed necessary for the sustainability of the planet.

Failure to do so meant "a death sentence for their communities"[29] for many small island states and African governments. At COP26, countries agreed to revisit and enhance their 2030 targets by the end of 2022. But few have done so. It is estimated that the carbon emissions reduction plans submitted at COP27 would "take less than 1 percent off projected global emissions in 2030" while "scientists say global emissions must be cut by 43 percent to hold temperature increases by the end of the decade to remain at 1.5C."[30] The countries that wanted to abolish the 1.5°C target failed; however, they did succeed in stopping the adoption of a clause to reach peak emissions by 2025 from being included in the agreement text. As a result of this partial victory, the 1.5°C limit cannot be attained by 2030.

Another crucial failure is the phasing down of all fossil fuel use. This was one of the main demands from many governments, activists, and nongovernmental organizations (NGOs). Although many expected such a decision, COP27 merely repeated COP26's call regarding "accelerating efforts towards the phasedown of unabated coal power and phase-out of inefficient fossil fuel subsidies."[31]

Louise Boyle and Saphora Smith report the reaction of those concerned:

> "We must emerge from Cop27 with a package of outcomes that keeps 1.5C alive and protects the world's vulnerable," said Tina Stege, the Marshall Islands' climate envoy. She was joined at the briefing by Mr Sharma and Jennifer Morgan, Germany's climate envoy, among others.

As regards the financial industry, the summit's text called on financial institutions to undertake necessary reforms, defining "their practices and priorities" so as to "ensure simplified access" to Sustainable Finance. The text also asked banks for a statement of a new vision that would render them "fit for the purpose of adequately addressing the global climate emergency."

This call may appear surprising at first since many banks in developed countries already have procedures meant to implement sustainable financing. However, as is the case with capitalist economies in general, many countries do not have such a financial system. Obviously, small island states and other vulnerable countries have no sources of funding. For them, the only chance to survive, if one exists, is to depend on multilateral development banks (MDBs) that would provide funds for catastrophic events such as flooding and rising sea levels. In such a situation, it is not difficult to perceive that such an undertaking would first be taken by MDBs; private financial institutions joining them subsequently, and only if they could make a profit.

In a press release following COP27, Friends of the Earth International included a quotation from their chair, Hemantha Withanage:

> The decision on carbon markets is deeply worrying. Whilst COP27 has temporarily delayed moves to put geoengineering, dangerous and untested technologies, and so-called nature-based solutions into carbon offset markets, we know these threats will rear their heads again. Carbon markets give cover for continued emissions by polluters, grabbing of land, forests and water from vulnerable communities, and violations of peoples' rights.[32]

Withanage enumerates climate-related risks and thus joins the club of critics. Nonetheless, she also mentions another crucial aspect, the social one:peoples' rights. When we talk about ESG, E almost always prevails even in regulations; the social aspect (S) is often secondary. When one talks about water, natural resources, and forests, the main questions are almost overlooked: whose water? whose natural resources? whose forests? to whom do they belong? and to whom should they belong? We will discuss further below. For now, I wish to note that E and S are interconnected. They cannot be separated if we want to live on a truly sustainable and just planet.

COP28 in Dubai

COP28 was held in Dubai at the end of 2023. If I start with the achievements, I will refer to the finalization of the Loss and Damage Fund. This fund is intended to help developing countries affected by climate change. According to the World Economic Forum, the United Arab Emirates and Germany each pledged $100 million, while the United Kingdom pledged a minimum of US$51 million. In addition, the European Union pledged US$245.39 million.[33] If we consider, for example, the US$105 billion in US aid to Israel and Ukraine,[34] it is easy to see what enormous sums of money are being spent to support developing countries when it comes to climate change! Another important point reported was the launch of the "Global Renewables and Energy Efficiency Pledge"[35] although anyone who reads the IEA's energy outlook and the IPCC's reports would easily notice that an increase in renewable energy is a must in order to keep global warming in line with the Paris Agreement. So is this launch an achievement or a delay? It seems the latter is the right answer to the question!

Remarks on COP26, COP27, and COP28 in Their Connection with the Overall Historical Development

Most of the facts recited above come from world financial news. Proponents of capitalist economies, whatever their stance, provide both positive and critical statements about all of these summits. To remember, in the *Grundrisse* and *Capital*, Marx mostly cited the statements of capitalist economists, their articles, as well as reports and reporting by the agents of classical political economy. His approach is remarkably fruitful as we undertake our own analysis based on their presentation of the subject matter. Checking the reliability of such reports, resolutions, and statements necessitates dialectics and immanent critique. That is to say, what Marx did in his time is still valid today. Officials' statements contain a surfeit of phenomena; a closer look and logical analysis, however, reveal what they actually plan and do. In opposition to postmodernist approaches, which undermined the function of the state and focused instead on governmentality and such, we are confronted with and experience an era in which the world is heating up, not only in terms of climate but politically as well.

In fact, a true climate change program must employ:

- A fast phase-out program of all fossil fuels: a concise and decisive commitment to phasing out fossil fuels by 2030 at the latest is essential to limit global warming to 1.5°C.
- Increased financial commitments: developed countries must increase their financial commitments and duties to compensate for the damage they have caused so far and support developing nations' climate efforts.
- A just transition: the transition to a carbon-neutral economy must be just and equitable, ensuring that vulnerable communities are supported without any conditions. Also, they must make their own decisions and define their wants and needs. It is not the case that they depend on the favor of the North. They have been suffering because of the North, and they should receive support because of the damage they face.
- Enhanced implementation: efficient mechanisms for monitoring and enforcing commitments are needed to close the gap between pledges and concrete action.

Nonetheless, I cannot say these can be expected by COPs in the current conditions as the main driver for capitalists is profitability and growth, including their nation-states, irrespective of what they say about politics, rights, ethics, wealth, and sustainability. And to maintain profitability and growth, they would not hesitate for a second to pollute the earth and pursue and employ aggressive political programs. Growth and profitability are their main goals; all other values and paradigms are secondary, playing only a complementary role in sustaining the profitability and growth of their firms.

Notes

1 Instead of CSR, readers would also notice that there is a trend to publish "Sustainability Report," "Non-financial Report," "Integrated Annual Report," and others which are all about disclosures of non-financial activities of corporations. Please pay special attention to the word "integrated"; it provides insights into how sustainability becomes an integral part of the financial system.

2 John Elkington, "The Triple Bottom Line," *Environmental Management: Readings and Cases* 2 (1997): 49–66.

3 Christine A. Mallin, "Introduction and Overview," in *Corporate Social Responsibility: A Case Study Approach*, ed. Christine A. Mallin (Northampton, MA: Edward Elgar, 2009), 1.

4 Andrea Melis, Silvia Carta, and Silvia Del Rio, "CSR and Integrated Triple Bottom Line Reporting in Italy: Case Study Evidence," in Mallin, *Corporate Social Responsibility*, 9.

5 Maria-Gabriella Baldarelli, Mara Del Baldo, and Caterina Ferrone, "The Relationships between CSR, Good Governance and Accountability in the Economy of Communion (EoC) Enterprises," in *Corporate Social Responsibility and Governance: Theory and Practice*, ed. Samuel O. Idowu, Claus Strue Frederiksen, Asli Yüksel Mermod, and Morten Ebe Juul Nielsen (London: Springer, 2015), 3–38.

6 Ibid.

7 Ibid., 30.

8 https://arcobaleno.net.

9 Archie B. Carroll, "Corporate Social Responsibility (CSR) and the Covid-19 Pandemic: Organizational and Managerial Implications," *Journal of Strategy and Management* 14, no. 3 (2021): 315–30.

10 See https://www.ipcc.ch/about/history/ for more details.
11 See https://www.ipcc.ch/report/sixth-assessment-report-working-group-i/.
12 See https://www.ipcc.ch/report/sixth-assessment-report-working-group-ii/.
13 Please see https://www.iea.org/reports/global-energy-and-climate-model/net-zero-emissions-by-2050-scenario-nze for more details and also to reach the link to the report.
14 One can read the rationale behind the update through https://www.iea.org/reports/world-energy-outlook-2022/an-updated-roadmap-to-net-zero-emissions-by-2050.
15 "From 1992 to 2022: The Evolution of Sustainable Finance," UNEP FI, https://www.unepfi.org/news/25th-anniversary/timeline.
16 "Climate: Get the Big Picture," UNFCCC, https://unfccc.int/resource/bigpicture/.
17 Colin Hunt, "Kyoto Protocol Fails: Get Ready for a Hotter World," *The Conversation*, November 15, 2012, https://theconversation.com/kyoto-protocol-fails-get-ready-for-a-hotter-world-10742.
18 United Nations, *The Millennium Development Goals Report 2015*, http://mdgs.un.org/unsd/mdg/Resources/Static/Products/Progress2015/English2015.pdf.
19 UNEP FI Climate Change Working Group, *CEO Briefing on Climate Change*, August 2002, https://www.unepfi.org/fileadmin/documents/CEO_briefing_climate_change_2002_en.pdf.
20 UNEP, https://www.unepfi.org/regions/africa-middle-east/redesigning-finance-for-sustainable-development/.
21 UNEP FI Positive Impact Initiative, "Rethinking Impact to Finance the SDGs: A Position Paper and Call to Action Prepared by Positive Impact Initiative," November 2018, 7, https://www.unepfi.org/wordpress/wp-content/uploads/2018/11/Rethinking-Impact-to-Finance-the-SDGs.pdf.
22 UNFCCC, Paris Agreement, 2015, https://unfccc.int/sites/default/files/english_paris_agreement.pdf.
23 BBC, "COP26: What was Agreed at the Glasgow Climate Conference?" November 15, 2021, https://www.bbc.com/news/science-environment-56901261.
24 Ibid.
25 Ibid.
26 Megan Rowling, "Analysis: COP27 Loss and Damage Fund Heralds 'New Dawn for Climate Justice,'" *Reuters*, November 20, 2022, https://www.reuters.com/business/cop/cop27-loss-damage-fund-heralds-new-dawn-climate-justice-2022-11-20/.
27 Ibid.
28 Ibid.

29 Louise Boyle and Saphora Smith, "Cop27 Outcomes: Key Takeaways from the Final Agreement," *The Independent*, November 21, 2022, https://www.independent.co.uk/climate-change/news/cop27-outcomes-summary-cop-27-b2229497.html.

30 Ibid.

31 Ibid.

32 Friends of the Earth International, "COP27 Outcome: Loss and Damage Fund Established in Historic First Step, but Other Outcomes Perilously Weak," https://www.foei.org/cop27-outcome/.

33 World Economic Forum, "COP28 Agrees to Establish Loss and Damage Fund for Vulnerable Countries," December 1, 2023, https://www.weforum.org/agenda/2023/12/cop28-loss-and-damage-fund-climate-change/.

34 CNN, "US Aid to Israel and Ukraine: Here's what's in the $105 billion National Security Package Biden Requested," November 28, 2023, https://edition.cnn.com/2023/10/20/politics/us-israel-ukraine-aid-package/index.html.

35 UNFCCC, "Summary of Global Climate Action at COP28—UNFCC," https://unfccc.int/sites/default/files/resource/Summary_GCA_COP28.pdf.

4

Limits and Inadequacies of Capitalism

In the previous chapters, our historical and logical analysis of finance demonstrated that the problem with the financial system is intrinsic. The capitalist system, with its inevitable tensions between money capital and industrial capital, is vulnerable to financial crises that arise from its own nature. In this chapter, I will take a closer look at this immanent problem of capitalism, especially in relation to Sustainable Finance. The proponents of capitalism want to dictate capitalist forms, offering sensational paradigms. They wish to sell these as the only reality possible. For them, the capitalist economy is the product of a natural tendency in human beings and in human society, and the only right and possible way to live. We must admit that many people accept this claim as an accurate description of our reality. Yet some of us continue to believe that a better society can be won by fundamentally transforming the existing capitalist order. To change the present reality, we must first understand what lies at the root of the problems within the capitalist system. We need to see how the capitalist community utilizes paradigms, how it structures its epistemology, and where the truth lies. To show the abstract universality of capitalism, so as to open the gates to a concrete universality, I will discuss the illusory aspects of capitalist paradigms: net-zero, financed emissions, deregulation and regulation, and financialization.

Net Zero Carbon Dioxide by 2050

Net zero is one of the most commonly touted paradigms for the decarbonization of the Earth. As a concept, it means the world will have net zero GHG emissions by 2050. Net zero implies that GHG emissions will occur by 2050 too, but they will be stored or captured so that the net amount of such emissions will be zero or negative. Let us explore this topic a bit more. It is important to grasp the main point of this concept.

McKinsey provides the following definition of net zero:

> Net zero is an ideal state where the amount of greenhouse gases (GHGs) released into the earth's atmosphere is balanced by the amount of GHGs removed. Decarbonization efforts are needed to reach net zero.[1]

This definition emphasizes reducing GHGs so that the quantities removed balance those that are released. Logically, the lower the amount of GHGs released, the less it is necessary to remove. This suggests that GHG removal technologies are adequate to compensate for the level of GHGs emitted—carbon neutrality.

The net zero emissions concept by 2050 stems from the 1.5°C limit on global warming compared to preindustrial levels. Two main organizations providing scenarios about the 1.5°C limit are the IPCC and the International Energy Agency (IEA). The 1.5°C scenarios are not the only ones; there are scenarios based well below 2°C—which were widely taken into consideration before tightening the limit—national pledges, and several others. On the other hand, there are differences among the 1.5°C scenarios; all can be seen in detail in IPCC's 6th Assessment Report (AR6), for instance. The AR6 is an extensive and continuous work that was published in three parts in 2021 and 2022, followed by a synthesis report in 2023. There are scenarios that project an overshoot to reach 1.5°C and others that entail low or no overshoot. Overshooting means that global warming will breach the 1.5°C barrier but then will go below that level. This is why scenarios taken by the financial industry are based on the low or no-overshoot scenario of the IPCC and the IEA, as though no overshooting will occur. As the documentation from the IPCC and IEA is very extensive, I will mainly focus on key points of the IPCC while referring to the IEA as well when necessary.

As 1.5°C with low or no overshooting is found to be the only viable one—even mandatory for those that set their climate targets—we should also understand its relationship to the global carbon budget. "Global carbon budget," as referred to earlier when talking about how it is consumed steadily, is the term used by the IPCC to describe the "maximum amount of cumulative net global anthropogenic carbon dioxide ($CO_{2)}$ emissions that would result in limiting global warming to a given level."[2] IPCC determined this budget as 500 $GtCO_2$ in the 6th Assessment Report.[3] Therefore, we can now have a simplified calculation to see how the "combat" against climate change is evolving. We should simply look at the annual estimates of $GtCO_2$ consumption. The IEA reported that CO_2 emissions in 2023 reached 37.4 Gt[4] (in other words, 37.4 billion tonnes!). And the world record was broken again. A striking recovery after Covid-19. Every time we break the world record, we break our own leg.

What these figures, projections, and estimates tell us is clear: if emissions continue on their current trajectory, our carbon budget will be used up in about 13 years (500 / 37.4 = 13.37). Assuming we have already consumed well since 2019 with reference to the baseline year in the AR6, the remaining carbon budget would now be about 200–300 Gt only. And when it is gone, it will be vulnerable to irreversible degradation of life on our planet. Can we overcome this danger? The IPCC AR6 and many other peer-reviewed articles say "yes." I believe there is such a possibility. However, it is obvious that we are doing almost exactly the opposite to destroy our lives, and more importantly, the lives of the next generations. So, I would argue that the net zero concept is an important concept "in itself," if I am allowed to use the terms of Kant (and Hegel) here. Is that achievable at all?

In her recent study of fossil fuels and net zero, Holly Jean Buck provides a richly informative account of the concept of net zero and explains its invention.[5] After the failures of the Copenhagen summit, Buck observes that the concept was revived by the 2015 Paris Agreement,[6] already noted above as a historically important event. And yet, despite all our knowledge and experiences about fossil fuels and despite what has been stressed at Conference of the Parties (COP)26, COP27, and COP28 about the phasing down of coal, this fossil fuel is still widely used. Contrary to what many people think, coal is not used by developing countries alone. For instance, the most advanced European economy, Germany, has been using coal for quite a long time. On the one hand, they seem to subscribe to the phasing out of coal, but on the other, they are gradually extending their use of it—capitalist paradigms and facts generally differ. To justify their intensive use of coal, the new excuse (or, say, deliverer) is the Russia-Ukraine conflict.

Reuters reported that 36.3 percent of the electricity supplied to the German power grids from July to September 2022 was generated by coal-fired power plants.[7] In the third quarter of 2021, it was 31.9 percent—a huge percentage itself. The German Green Party has long been critical of the extensive use of coal; however, the German government appears not to care much about its opposition. In early 2022, German Chancellor Olaf Scholz explained that this increase—in both oil- and coal-fired power plants—was the result of the war between Russia and Ukraine. He said it would be temporary, just as the war itself could only be temporary.[8] Scholz himself said: "it is only for a very short time."[9] Ironically, Scholz and his government are among those doing everything to prolong the war and decline to act as intermediaries to end the conflict. Although Scholz's statement seems, logically, to mean "the increase in oil and coal use will last a very short time, because the war will quickly be over," in fact, as of December 2022, the circumstances indicate that this is not true.

Our deconstruction and reconstruction of Scholz's words clearly show that he defends the use of coal and oil because of the war. He obviously falls into a fallacy, as revealed by the discrepancy between his actions and words. Furthermore, we should ask why he and the German government favor the increased use of coal. The reason is simple: because it is now cheaper! Strangely enough, even the fiercest climate activists defended—if conditionally—the increased use of coal. Karsten Smid, of Greenpeace Germany, stated that it is perhaps the best solution in the circumstance, but demanded that the government offset the increased carbon emissions by reducing emissions elsewhere.[10]

Such news reports, intentionally or inadvertently, conceal another detail: they treat this increase as though prior use was not itself too intense. Even though one clearly states that 31.9 percent of electricity was generated from coal in the third quarter of 2021, it does not inquire further into this percentage. In fact, Germany is one of the largest coal-producing countries in the world. It was ranked eighth in the world. Jessica Dillinger states the following:

> Germany is still the biggest producer of brown coal but closed down its last hard coal mines in 2018. A phase-out of coal power is goal in Germany. However, coal still has 35.3 percent share in German power production. It is still 6th in the world in terms of reserves and 4th in the world in terms of consumption.[11]

There is no new sharp increase in coal use in Germany. The country's past shows that coal-fired energy generation was remarkably high. Germany is not the only country that has increased its use of fossil fuels. The United Kingdom, for instance, is no different.[12] We can understand why these countries are increasing the volume of fossil fuels, but we should not accept their mystifications of facts. "This winter" does not give the whole story. We need to undertake a deconstruction in order to perceive what is hidden behind this phenomenon. Also consider Olaf Scholz's assertion that the war will be over soon. Basing the claim that the increase in fossil fuel use will be of short duration on this pronouncement is to offer an abstract argument. Besides, without a major change in the policies of Western countries, and the Anglo-American powers especially, there is little to suggest that the war will end any time soon. On the contrary, these powers engage in more brutal activities to prolong the war. Back in February 2022, Germany, under the guise of allocating 2 percent of its Gross Domestic Product (GDP) to defense spending to meet NATO requirements, announced that it would build a special fund—not a climate fund this time—with a pledge of €100 billion: a wonderful offset to supply the army with better equipment.[13] Moreover, the explanation given in this story is not true: to meet NATO requirements, about €70 billion would suffice. In addition, Germany already has the seventh-best funded military sector in the world, its funding climbing to approximately €50.3 billion in 2022 compared to €32.5 billion in 2011.[14]

Let us recap. On the one hand, Germany—along with other countries—increases its use of fossil fuels, including the most polluting fossil fuel of all: coal. It claims that this is a temporary measure and will not last long. On the other hand, Germany allocates huge funds to top up its military defense, nearly doubling its spending in ten years. This clearly demonstrates two facts: (a) Germany would not hesitate to seize on any excuse to pollute the environment, and (b) in contrast to official statements, Germany is preparing plans for a huge military buildup beyond "this winter." Now, we can better understand why 2025 was not accepted as the peak year of carbon emissions, regardless of their statements. Let us put ourselves in the shoes of the officials of these countries. German and British officials tell us at a COP summit that we need to determine the year when emissions should peak. In the evening, we go to our hotel room and watch the news. We see that huge military investments have been secured, the closure of coal power plants has been suspended, new coal plants are given permission to operate, and even those who defend the phase-out of coal justify its use. What would we say when we meet them the next day? These controversies and the German increase in thermal coal use infuriated Greta Thunberg, the famous climate activist. She criticized German authorities for planning to shut down nuclear power plants while increasing coal use.[15] Who would ever have expected Thunberg would defend nuclear power over thermal coal? This is exactly our paradox today: in despair, we embrace the less harmful alternative.

The reason for the increase in fossil fuel use sheds light on capitalist economies. The main driver when capitalists employ an energy source—or any type of production—is profit, even though they emphasize the green economy, sustainability, and so on. In other words, if they do not see one type of production as equally profitable to another that relies on dirty fossil fuels, they do not care enough about carbon emissions and such to adopt it.

We can now better see the remarkable character of Hegelian and Marxian concepts that—dialectically—tie appearance to essence in the example of coal use. Beneath the surface there always lies what, in fact, is being done. To overcome the illusions of capitalist realism, one must always try to lift the veil to reveal what the paradigm hides.

McKinsey states that although "power, oil and gas, and transport industries" are most often cited as the biggest emitters of GHGs, all industries should pledge to achieve net zero targets. They define decarbonization as the "mitigation, cessation, or reduction of carbon in the atmosphere. It is achieved by switching to energy sources or materials that emit less carbon, often from high carbon-emitting fossil fuels and by counteracting any carbon that is emitted."[16]

As seen earlier, the Paris Agreement stipulates that efforts should not exceed 1.5°C above preindustrial levels. To achieve this goal, net greenhouse gas emissions should be limited in order to prevent extreme heat and consequences such as deforestation, flooding, sea level rise, and other disasters. This could be seen as a decarbonization effort. As already noted, many countries and organizations have pledged to undertake decarbonization efforts. Many companies have also committed themselves to these efforts, claiming to have taken net zero transition measures and steps. However, since the 1990s, these efforts have not met with success. The current net zero drive is likely to fail as well, as it relies on unfeasible projections—for example, planting from 25 to 80 percent of our planet's biomass or carbon capture and storage at enormous levels.[17] The abstract universality of political economy still dominates, and illusion still holds sway. We can see the dilemma at work between humans and nature. Humans' alienation from their own essence drives them to manipulate and destroy ecosystems, turning forests into mere vehicles for carbon capture. That there is much more to discover in biodiversity apparently no longer occurs to the majority of humans.[18]

On the mountain of appearances—the expression is taken from Hegel[19]—we see commitments, efforts, targets. Nonetheless, we should inquire further into what lies beyond these appearances. The Network for Greening the Financial System (NGFS) presents itself as "a group of central banks and supervisors committed to sharing best practices, contributing to the development of climate—and environment—related risk management in the financial sector and mobilizing mainstream finance to support the transition toward a sustainable economy."[20] The NGFS provides climate scenarios and analyzes and forecasts possible future outcomes. It provides detailed analyses produced by some central banks and academic institutes working together. Here, beyond the appearances, we discover a statement by the NGFS that current policies will not be enough to achieve net zero GHG emissions by 2050, and that there is no chance of meeting the 1.5°C target—or even the 2°C. The scenario analysis demonstrates that emissions will continue to increase until 2080 and the temperature of our planet, in the 2090s, will increase by 3°C compared to preindustrial levels.[21] In other words, despite the grand paradigms and "green statements" offered, the actuality in terms of decarbonization falls far short of impeding global heating. There is something truly disturbing here. Many financial institutions have policies regarding high GHG-emitting industries. Many banks have coal phase-out policies, restrictions on oil and gas policies, such as phasing out Arctic drilling and deep-water exploration. Hence, to claim simply that banks do not care or do not take action is one-sided. However, it is debatable whether such measures are adequate to achieve a decarbonized world. Yet I would like to discuss another point related to the net zero paradigm.

As we have seen, many corporations include commitments, strategies, and disclosures in sustainability reports. Major banks' financing strategies consider ESG—sustainability—criteria. Nonetheless, we can see, based on the NGFS scenarios and other sources, that these efforts will not achieve the net zero target by 2050. On the contrary, if current policies and practices do not change, we can expect an even hotter planet.

Power, oil and gas, and transport (also known as mobility) are widely accepted as among the biggest GHG-emitting industries. After these, steel and cement, real estate, and agriculture (including food and forestry) are considered to be the highest GHG-emitting sectors.[22] The main concern is fossil fuels: 83 percent of overall CO_2[23] emissions are caused by fossil fuels. Historically beginning with coal and expanding later to oil and gas companies, these industries emit huge quantities of CO_2. The power sector, which uses fossil fuels for power generation, also emits high levels of CO_2. Mobility is no different because it uses vehicles with internal combustion engines. Steel and cement production techniques contribute a great deal to emissions (14 percent[24]) even though steel is itself a green product. Forestry causes carbon emissions from "land clearing and deforestation."[25]

Carbon emissions are inevitable; they are caused either by the production process or the end products themselves (e.g., passenger vehicles). Industries and organizations endeavor to deal with carbon emissions by using different techniques—renewable energy, hydrogen use, carbon capture, carbon storage, and so on. Innovation and technological advances will play a significant role in the overall reduction of GHGs.

To better understand the targets, we should first determine their basic characteristics. This requires us first to understand the role of decision-makers in the productive forces. We can only grasp the content and meaning of the targets if we have a clear idea of whose targets they are. With the appearance of domination in human history, a minority of people took decisions that were binding on those in their orbit. Masters and slaves, lords and servants, bourgeoisie and workers: these are different forms of social relationships pertaining to different societies; however, a constant runs through them all: oppressor and oppressed.

At the beginning of bourgeois society, there were occasions when a great number of people participated in society-related decisions. This was when the bourgeoisie defended civil society, property rights, and demanded that the state recognize the members of society. I would call this the liberal era. However, this era did not last long. Although nation-states emerged and, to a great extent, swept over the Earth (bourgeois) nation by nation, the liberal soul faded away. This is to say that we must keep in mind that concepts such as sustainability and net zero are paradigms belonging to the ruling classes and their vehicles. Max Ajl argues that only a very small number of economies in the North are beginning to decouple GDP growth from the growth in CO_2; however, this is rather deceptive, he adds, as the carbon emissions counted do not take consumption into account but only production.[26] Ajl continues:

> in theory, China, Vietnam, Bangladesh, and the Philippines could be the site of nearly every polluting bit of industrial production currently occurring in Finland and France, while the entire WTO trading architecture and imperialist political engineering, and unequal exchange through which value and wealth concentrate in the North, remain intact. Chunks of high-end programming and marketing, sophisticated work on robotics, and patents could remain in the North. The result would "decouple" GDP from CO_2 in the affluent core. Such a sleight of hand is based on imperial trading architecture and carbon accounting procedures. In fact, the trend towards decreasing impact of northern development on northern environments has occurred alongside increasing impact of northern development on the southern environments. Four to eight percent of air pollution in China in 2006, for example, was linked to exports of products to the US.[27]

It requires an analysis that moves from appearance to essence (from the abstract to the concrete) to reveal the truth behind what we see in our immediate surroundings. Beyond appearances, the reality is that the grand net zero paradigm relies on technology that does not yet exist,[28] or else on production that costs much more than that used by competitors. Therefore, capitalist reality, implicitly, relies on a better future based on the possibility of a better reality! On the one hand, capitalism tells us that we live in the only reality possible; on the other hand, it endeavors to make us believe the future will be better. Nor is this done in a fair way. In 2021, Brett Wilkins observed that big companies—major polluters—encouraged reputable universities to conduct net zero research but retained the right to check their results before completion, and even to employ their own staff as part of the research team![29] How, in such a situation, can we expect any research that would contradict their interests? So, perception arises from such background plays. What we need is a true net zero. If the rich restrain their GHG emissions, it will seem that the world would not have to wait until 2050 for a carbon-free planet. Such illusory shifts conceal the discrepancy intrinsic to net zero, and, more broadly, to capitalism. Now that we have addressed the illusory nature of capitalism, let us inquire into the epistemological stance of the world of finance.

Epistemological Issue

Financial regulations and textbooks contain a lot of talk about having knowledgeable investors. They mention that every investor, especially small individuals, should understand financial investments and the risks involved. This is fine rhetoric, but such investors have never existed in significant numbers. The first global sustainability benchmark was launched by Dow Jones in 1999. Investors looking for (a) profitable companies and (b) companies that abide by the principles of sustainable development use this sustainability index as a guide. Both companies and individual investors had a benchmark they could use to find profitable companies that followed ESG principles. This kind of knowledge seems helpful to all types of investors, but it is, by its very nature, insufficient. It asks investors to rely on the index's classification—but always with the caveat that investors should do their own due diligence!

Knowledge is a major issue in the field of finance. It is no different in the field of Sustainable Finance. The classical definition of epistemology is to define knowledge as "justified true belief" (JTF). Therefore, the position of an investor who buys a so-called green asset is based on their own JTF. However, their justification of the belief that the purchased asset is green is abstract. The seller (the financial institution) simply labels the asset as green, and the justification is done. However, this does not mean that the asset is truly green or even that the asset is much different from the classical financial assets sold on the market. Knowledge is vulnerable to being abstract, one-sided, and inadequate.

Investing in ESG funds is deemed a socially responsible investment (SRI). SRI has grown in popularity in tandem with the ESG paradigm. Investors drawn to SRI usually take into account environmental, social, and governmental aspects. However, because there is no consensus on the content of these terms, what constitutes an ESG fund and what constitutes an SRI investor remains rather abstract. For example, when an investor looks for companies in which to invest, corporate annual reports, mass media reports, third-party ESG ratings, and the like will be the primary sources of information. The investor would still buy a company's assets, assuming they are green, if the company promoted ESG through its commitments, advertisements, and campaigns. In January 2022, Bloomberg Intelligence reported: "ESG could reach more than $41 trillion in assets by the end of 2022 and $50 trillion by 2025."[30] Given such vast sums, greenwashing through misrepresentation is endemic. This may seem like an extravagant claim, but the following examples will make the case more convincing.

One of the cases is about IKEA. The Carpathian region of Ukraine is known for its rich timber resources. Its forests are a home for wolves, bears, and other animals. However, an Earthsight investigation in the year 2020 discovered that IKEA wanted to harvest some of the wood in the region for its beech chairs.[31] The Forest Stewardship Council (FSC) certified that the use of the wood from the region was legal, but Earthsight discovered that it was not. IKEA has a very good reputation when it comes to ESG,[32] and the FSC is the preeminent accrediting body.[33]

Innocent Drinks, a company owned by Coca-Cola, promoted a green world in its 2022 advertising, featuring cuddly and endearing animals singing and preaching about recycling to save the planet. The ads were banned by the Advertising Standards Authority (ASA),[34] the United Kingdom's independent regulator. Coca-Cola is rated as a "medium risk" company by Sustainalytics and is ranked thirty-first among food and beverage companies out of 603 companies rated.[35]

Another striking example would be from the transportation industry. We all remember Volkswagen's case in the United States. In September 2015, the company, after accusations of using a device on cars that run on diesel engines, admitted to the use of such a device that helped them pass emission tests. This software, when emissions tests were being conducted, was able to show fewer emissions than the actual ones.

In the automotive industry, such cases might be continuing, not necessarily through such devices. Lab tests and real-world cases do not match each other. A very good way of monitoring how we are deceived in terms of knowledge can be tracked through the real-life emissions published by the European Environment Agency (EEA). The monitoring of such emissions (real-world) versus lab tests actually finds its roots in the EU Regulation 2019/631. This was a good step from the EU to compare what has been declared as the result of the World Harmonized Light Vehicle Test Procedure (WLTP)—laboratory mandatory tests—and what happens in real life. The results published by the EEA were striking. There was a gap of 21.1 percent for petrol cars. This percentage was 17.1 for diesel cars. Hold tight, for hybrid vehicles, it was 239 percent for petrol and 317 percent for diesel cars.[36] So, if we calculate scenarios and pathways based on WLTP lab data, how far are we from reality? What is the position of such knowledge? Such questions probably would not even qualify as good questions as their answers are very obvious!

Such cases are widespread. For us, the important question is: How responsible is an investor who, after carrying out due diligence, invests in these companies? This is the epistemological fallacy of knowledge related to investment. Ethics and responsibility are always secondary in a world driven by profitability and growth. Individual investors can do their best to invest in ESG assets, but there will always be the danger of misinformation, misuse, and manipulation. This problem inheres in the deceptive nature of the financial system, regardless of the choices made by ethical investors. There is no possibility of equal knowledge in the capitalist economy; this is the hidden fact that lies behind the rhetoric.

Investment and Recent Events

Back in March 2020, the disruptive effect of the Covid-19 pandemic on financial markets was enormous. It is still fresh in our minds how we were all gradually forced to stay indoors, to wear masks even in public parks, and how work-related social problems reached an apogee. Strangely enough, in Austria, we were initially not even allowed to go to parks, and then slowly, when the country was experiencing about 500–600 cases per day, we were able to go. In the summer of 2022, when cases in Austria ranged from 5 to 15,000 per day, people were allowed to go almost everywhere, maskless.[37] The financial situation was somewhat similar; in a speculative environment where an enormous amount of money is in circulation, a simple disruption can have significant consequences.

In March 2020, US hedge funds suffered big losses.[38] A hedge fund is a vehicle that seeks to achieve the highest rate of return that alternative investments can offer. Hedge fund losses are a striking example of how "bets" in financial markets can impact the overall situation during such times. The problem in March 2020 lay with the investments of US hedge funds, which managed US$2.4 trillion on behalf of their wealthy investors.[39] The way to gain the highest rate of return with the least amount of risk, at that time, was to invest, using leverage, in the futures of interest rates using funds borrowed in repo transactions. For the lay reader, "leverage" can be read as "theoretically unlimited investment." However, interest rates changed direction, to the cost of hedge funds and their investors, when markets were hit by Covid-19.

The Federal Reserve Bank (the Fed) acted appropriately and in a timely manner to solve the problem by buying government bonds in significant amounts; without such a measure, the trouble could have easily spread. As a result, banks and financial institutions that lent money to hedge funds were able to weather the situation without major problems. Thus, interest rates reverted to the initially estimated levels, and the crisis was overcome, with only some hedge funds collapsing. I used the words "appropriately" and "timely" in reference to the Fed's purchase because otherwise there would have been a much greater collapse. However, if interest rates move in line with expectations, who is the beneficiary? Wealthy investors and the hedge funds themselves. The Dodd-Frank Act, passed after the subprime crisis, was designed to prevent government bailouts: the Fed's action is in obvious violation of its provisions. There are still critics of the 2008 bailouts; according to them, the market should have been allowed to collapse freely so that a new (and still free) market could rise from its ashes. These are the usual aspects of finance capital: violating their own rules, supporting capital at the expense of those who do not have it, to secure the essence of the production of capital under the guise of global claims of justice, equality, and the like. Once again, this hedge fund example illustrates the insatiable nature of money capital and how the financial system acts to save financial actors—sometimes letting them go bankrupt for the greater good, that is, the financial system as a whole—and always at the expense of the common people.

Capitalism is a system that drives growth and profitability. Growth is a prerequisite for profitability. For sustainable profitability, there should always be sustainable growth in the capitalist sense of the economy. On the other hand, we have seen that the intrinsic nature of the capitalist economy is vulnerable to crises: in the past, production-related crises, and more recently, financial ones. We have also demonstrated that the dominance of the financial system has led to crises in the financial sphere.

One could argue that growth and profitability could also be sustainable through the sustainable use of natural resources and the responsible control of investments and financing. This is the deceptive "human face" of sustainability presented by the dominant forces. When it comes to sustainability, the first elements to be questioned are growth and profitability per se. The activities of Sustainable Finance are an indication of where the markets are today. If we look beyond the jargon and the mantras, we will see the finer details of what "sustainability" means.

To reveal the true nature of capitalist sustainability, let us turn to a few other activities in published reports by UNEP FI. In January 2021, UNEP FI and the European Banking Federation produced a report entitled "Testing the application of the EU Taxonomy to core banking products: High level recommendations."[40] This report assessed how and according to what measure the EU Taxonomy on Sustainable Activities could be applied to core banking products. It recommended the extensive use of the EU Taxonomy. Once applied, banks would label, promote, and disclose their products. In March 2021, another report on sustainable ocean recovery was published.[41] This report provided tools to guide banks, insurers, and investors about how to finance (or invest in) the so-called blue economy in a sustainable way. More reports appeared in the busy year 2021. In April 2021, one on climate target setting appeared.[42] This report outlined key principles for aligning with the targets of the Paris Agreement. Finally, in July 2021, another report on the impact on investor decision-making came out,[43] which also included an outline of sustainability and relevant accounting. This report consisted of legal analyses of eleven jurisdictions, allowing investors to consider the impact of their activities. These eleven jurisdictions included the usual suspects—big economies—as well as South Africa. The report also provided a set of options for policymakers to facilitate sustainable investments—if there were any. In practical terms, it amounted to a call to change the legal duties of investors.

These reports illustrate that, for capitalists, sustainability could be achieved with the involvement of financial institutions. The latter should join the project of sustainability—in the capitalist understanding of the term—so that the transformation can be accomplished. Transforming the planet to a sustainable economy, in fact, means transforming the capitalist system, and its financial players especially, so that they can enjoy growth and profitability according to their own image of sustainability. Sustainability, as a new paradigm of capitalism, is an illusion. Sustainability will not be possible as long as growth and profitability are the primary goals. This is an immanent limitation of the system and will never change unless the system takes its place in history as a past form.

Growth and Distribution of Wealth

The coming of the Industrial Revolution signified the beginning of economic growth in the modern era. The widely held view is that it originated in England toward the end of the eighteenth century. The steam engine marked a turning point in the sense that it enabled mass production on a much greater scale compared to previous modes of production. Nonetheless, the enormous use of coal involved came at a dramatic cost, one that would be felt, perhaps, for centuries. Coal use for steam-powered production made the factory system more efficient. The principal industries involved in mass production were textiles and steel, the latter used to produce machines for production. Hence, with the significantly reduced costs of transportation (e.g., freight), international trade grew at an accelerated rate. Coal also contributed to economic gain through its use in producing fertilizers. Jeffrey Sachs points out that other mid-nineteenth-century technology innovations were the tycoon and, more significantly, the telegraph.[44] Thus, transportation and communication technologies facilitated links to other markets and helped the owners of capital form economies of scale that offered cost advantages in the production phase. When technology and production capacity are actual, infrastructure adapts accordingly. The Suez Canal came into operation in 1869 and greatly reduced transportation costs. Another wave came at the end of the century. It was the expansion of the power industry and the advent of the internal combustion engine. This was followed by the boost in agricultural production from nitrogen-based fertilizers[45] at the beginning of the twentieth century.

The important point about these historical developments is that modes of production advance through technological innovations, which bring about relational improvements in other sectors, such as communication, transportation, and infrastructure. It is certainly worthwhile to dwell on this point to gain a better understanding of the liberal development of capitalism. Nonetheless, I will refrain from doing so since it would deviate too far from the focus of this study. A relevant observation, however, is that a causal relation between modes of production and relevant industries emerged at the dawn of the modern era.

Growth in itself does not say much about economic conditions. One needs to analyze how growth in the economy is distributed. If a mechanism existed that distributed growth fairly, we would perhaps not have much reason to talk about injustice and social inequality. We have already examined the way that capitalists extract surplus from the production process, from the workers who work extra time for them. Subsequently, economic growth favors those who own capital, whereas those who sell their labor power do not benefit equally from this growth. For capitalists, growth makes the working class wealthier as well, although they would admit that the distribution of wealth is imperfect. When the working class benefits from growth, injustice may well be hidden—until growth is interrupted. And the interruption of growth is inevitable in a capitalist economy. Such was the case in the years following the signing of Bretton Woods. In fact, for almost three decades after 1943, the developed economies enjoyed remarkable growth, and one must admit that the condition of the working class improved. Nonetheless, such a temporary, though dramatic, rise does not alter the essence of the capitalist economy. When growth slows and recession follows, the cold truth of the system's essence takes over, demonstrating that those who pay in these conditions are the members of the working class.

Economic growth lies at the heart of capitalism. It is impossible to convince a capitalist to invest in an industry that fails to grow. The question is whether it is possible to have sustainable growth in the capitalist mode of production. Advocates of sustainable growth and Sustainable Finance, who claim that a sustainable economy is possible, actually defend the possibility and reality of growth. Nonetheless, I have a great deal of doubt about the possibility and the feasibility of their argument. This forms the basic argument of this chapter and its subsections.

It is now time to discuss the oscillation between deregulation and regulation. Once the nature of this oscillation is explained, its hidden aspect will reveal itself as the essence of the system and reveal the truth behind the seeming conflict.

Financed Emissions

Financial institutions are under increasing pressure from their own customers, regulators, activists, and stewards to be more transparent about their role in climate change and other sustainability issues. Many financial institutions recognize their critical role in the sustainability transition of the real economy, particularly with respect to climate change. They are increasingly integrating environmental, social, and governance (ESG) criteria into their investment and lending decisions, supporting initiatives that reduce emissions and promote sustainable practices. In doing so, they aim to drive the transition to a greener and more sustainable future. Many are committed to reducing the carbon footprint of their operations and, more importantly, the emissions associated with the way they finance and invest, the so-called "financed emissions." As a first step in building trust that financial institutions are integrating climate change into their core business of providing and allocating capital, banks need to quantify financed emissions, as they do with sustainability ratings.

In our data-driven era, financed emissions do not say anything unless they are measured. We have two questions in hand: What constitutes the financed emissions of banks? And how are these emissions measured? When we answer these questions, will we be able to build upon them other questions and outcomes?

While banks may not directly generate significant emissions from their own operations, their lending and investment activities can have a significant impact on greenhouse gas emissions. These indirect emissions, called financed emissions, represent the carbon footprints of bank-financed projects and companies. Financed emissions, which are indirect emissions that occur in a company's value chain, are typically categorized as Scope 3 emissions under the Greenhouse Gas Protocol. For banks, these emissions can result from a wide range of activities, including loans to fossil fuel companies, investments in industries with high emissions, and mortgages on buildings that are not energy efficient.

Measuring financed emissions is a complex task that requires assessing the carbon footprint of different projects and companies in a bank's portfolio. One of the most widely recognized and used accounting standards for measuring emissions is the Greenhouse Gas Protocol ("GHG Protocol"). The GHG Protocol provides guidance to companies on how to measure their emissions. When it comes to banks, the Partnership for Carbon Accounting Financials ("PCAF") standard has been developed to calculate these emissions. In other words, we can argue that the PCAF is the GHG Protocol's derivative for banks to measure their financed emissions. To measure their financed emissions, financial institutions typically collect or purchase data from suppliers on the financed activity, estimate the associated emissions using sector-specific emission factors, and allocate the emissions to the bank based on its proportional share of the financing. One thing to keep in mind for financial institutions is to consider a bank's own direct emissions, such as fossil fuel combustion, vehicle fleet, etc. (Scope 1—direct emissions). Consider also the bank's purchased indirect emissions, such as utilities (Scope 2—indirect emissions). And compare this to the bank's financing and investment activities (Scope 3—value chain). As you can imagine, Scope 3 is much larger than the sum of Scope 1 and Scope 2. To give a clear idea, it would be useful to mention that the financed emissions of financial institutions were about 700 times higher than their own emissions as reported in April 2021.[46] Simply put, a bank may own a thousand cars while financing a million. This is exactly what the PCAF provides standards and guidance for: to guide banks to measure and potentially disclose their financed emissions. The measurement of financed emissions is still a work in progress, and there is ongoing debate as to which methodologies are the most accurate and comprehensive. However, financial institutions are moving toward more transparent and standardized reporting practices due to the growing recognition of the importance of these emissions.

Increasingly, banks are disclosing the emissions that they finance in their sustainability reports and are setting targets to reduce their carbon footprint. This means aligning their investments with the goals of the Paris Agreement, including limiting global warming to well below 1.5°C. Banks aim to contribute to the transition to a low-carbon economy and mitigate the effects of climate change by measuring and addressing their financed emissions. Also, financial institutions are required to disclose their Scope 3 GHG financed emissions. As we explained earlier, Scope 3 of a financial institution encompasses Scope 1, 2, and 3 emissions of their clientele. In other words, it includes emissions from the entire value chain of the clientele, not just the direct emissions of financial institutions.

Let me be clear: it would be so one-sided to argue that banks are not doing anything to decarbonize the planet. On the contrary, they are making great efforts. Most of them have a phase-out strategy to get out of the coal business by 2030, to reduce the financing of fossil fuel combustion such as upstream oil, and have a greenhouse gas emission reduction path for 2030 and 2050. In general, they define and disclose their sectoral climate targets based on the International Energy Agency's (IEA) Net Zero Scenario (NZE 2050). The Net-Zero Banking Alliance mentions that its members cover 41 percent of global banking assets.[47]

However, despite these efforts, there are several drawbacks to setting financed emissions targets. In short, this is due to the mixing of apples and pears into the same basket. Let us now discuss the dynamics of financed emissions targets and see how healthy and meaningful the whole exercise is.

Financed Emission Targets: Overarching Pathways and Sectoral Pathways

It is not an easy task for financial institutions to set easy-to-set targets based on scenarios and pathways. The main challenge appears especially when financial institutions try to set targets derived from sectoral benchmarks. There are two main approaches for setting targets: (a) so-called "abstract contraction method" (ACA) and (b) "sectoral decarbonization approach" (SDA). Both approaches have their advantages and setbacks; let us discuss the main particularities of both.

The ACA is also known as the overall portfolio approach or overarching target approach. It takes the whole portfolio into consideration and sets one common target for the whole portfolio (e.g., 40 percent financed emissions decrease by 2030 compared to 2020 levels). The SDA, on the other hand, takes a specific sector into account and defines emission intensity decrease for the target year (e.g., steel emission intensity to be 1.1 tCO_2 per tonne of steel by 2030 compared to 1.5 tCO_2 per tonne of steel in 2020).

The ACA might follow several parameters such as national pledges, global GHG emissions benchmarks, a specific region or country's emission decrease for the target year, and so on. For instance, a financial institution can reach out to a 1.5°C compliant scenario under which it can find regional or national emission decrease levels per region and country and then calculate its own scenario's pathway per region or country. Then, it can compare these emission reduction benchmarks to the national pledges of countries and see the gap between them. At the moment, national pledges are far from being 1.5°C compliant; so, most probably, the bank would have to use the benchmarks it would find in the relevant scenario. It is not a bad method, but it assumes that the bank's own scenario aligns with the national or regional pathways, which will generally not be a good match. To overcome this relatively high-level and top-down approach, the SDA can be used for a bottom-up method. Will it, however, solve the problem?

It cannot solve the problem; it can only minimize it, although this minimization is not guaranteed. Why? First, banks set their climate targets based on physical emission intensities. Physical emission intensity is the amount of CO_2 emitted per relevant commodity, and so on. For example, if a steel producer's operation emits 1.5 tons of CO_2 per ton of steel, then the physical emission intensity of steel in this case is 1.5 tCO_2/t steel. On the other hand, the financed emission intensity is the amount of CO_2 of steel per financed activity. For example, if a bank finances a steel producer for €10 million and the result of this financing is fifty thousand tons of CO_2 (Scope 1—direct emissions), then the financed emission intensity is 10,000,000/50,000 = 200 tCO_2/t steel. This means that for every €1 million financed, the bank's financing causes 200 tons of carbon dioxide emissions.

The problem is that reductions in physical emission intensities do not guarantee the same percentage reduction in financed emissions. For example, the IEA projects that direct emissions from steel will fall to 1.07 tCO_2/t steel by 2030. Given the physical emissions intensity of 1.41 tCO_2 in 2022,[48] this represents a decrease of 24 percent (1.07/1.41) from 2022 to 2030. However, there is no single methodology that can justify that this percentage will have the same effect on financed emissions. No bank can be sure that its steel-related financed emissions will also decrease by 24 percent from 2022 to 2030. So how will banks set their financed emissions targets? Will they simply continue to set their targets based on physical emission intensities, or will they estimate the same reduction ratio and reflect the same ratio in their financed emission intensity targets? This is where the black box comes in.

Because SDAs take emission intensities into account, but what emissions are we talking about here? Physical emissions! Therefore, even if SDAs are calculated carefully, customer data collected with good efforts and proper estimate values are employed, this reduction target is in itself a target for the reduction of "physical" emission intensities. This is exactly what the Science Based Targets Initiative (SBTi) and others offer as decarbonization pathways. Therefore, although a granular approach for a given sector can be applied, how can we guarantee that the physical emission intensity decrease has the same impact on financed emission intensities and financed emissions? We cannot! This is the setback of the SDA, and it seems this topic is rather kept aside for discussion. In an industry, if there is a method widely accepted, to oppose and revise it is not a very feasible option as it may expose the quality of the method applied to the whole sector since it is a questionable structure. Such things are not welcome!

Beyond all this data fetish that gives the impression that everything is measured, lie the facts: total energy sector CO_2 emissions were up 1.1 percent in 2023. Instead of the rapid decline needed to meet the global climate goals of the Paris Climate Accord, CO_2 emissions reached 37.4 Gt in 2023—another record high, as reported by the IEA.[49] The IEA also states that the growth in emissions is mainly due to increasing demand for coal in both emerging and developed economies[50]—a hard fact, even though many financial institutions have policies to phase out coal by 2030.

In the area of financed emissions, we are immersed in a world of estimates that are presented with a veneer of truth unless we dig deeper into the details of the reports and realize that most of the data points are based on estimates. Financial institutions seeking to demonstrate their commitment to sustainability, or those required to disclose their funded emissions, rely heavily on this estimated emissions data to quantify their environmental impact. However, this reliance on data, while seemingly objective and accurate, can often obscure the complex reality of carbon footprints. This data fetishism, as sociologist Jean Baudrillard might describe it, creates a simulacrum—a representation that has become more real than reality itself in his own words: "Illusion is no longer possible, because the real is no longer possible."[51]

Having discussed the above points, we are again faced with the problem of over-quantification. This quantification fetish pushes us toward measurable facts that we cannot properly measure. This creates two dangers: oversimplification of phenomena and reliance on what has been fabricated. Disclaimers are popular, saying that estimates cannot match facts, but then no one discusses the facts. What we need instead is something clear and concise, like phasing out funding for the coal industry by 2030. Why is this clear exit policy not applied to other pollutants such as fossil fuels? The answer is now clearer: because if such a policy does not come into effect, the opportunity to generate growth and profit will not be missed. The fetish of quantification contributes to the transformation of the financial system. It generates paradigms as if great efforts and achievements were on the way, but in fact, this fetish hides the real growth of greenhouse gas emissions as of today, and unless this ideological mask is torn, it will continue to hide the actualizing failure.

The issue with financed emissions is not that banks do not engage with them. On the contrary, there is an increasing number of financial institutions that disclose their financed emissions and financed emissions targets. They even disclose whether such targets are on track. However, it is not an effort that can be achieved through the synthesis of financed CO_2 per €1 million or US$1 million. If the real economy and its regulatory framework do not change their direction, it will just be an exercise of numbers and simulated projections from the side of financial institutions. Financed emissions are likely to remain a paradigm unless the core system changes.

Deregulation vs. Regulation—Two Sides of the Same Coin

When people talk about regulation, they almost invariably mean the financial rules that govern the market, allowing state intervention when necessary. However, when we talk about deregulation, the matter is not so simple, because deregulation can also mean regulation from a historical perspective. A few historical facts will help explain what I mean. This will help us gain a better understanding of the implicit mechanism behind the regulation-deregulation oscillation.

Historically, we see that the economic growth of advanced nations—advanced in economic and industrial terms—was interrupted by the First World War. Beyond and following such catastrophic events, there was a greater likelihood of economic recoveries, which are debatable in themselves, being interrupted—in this sequence, by the Great Depression and the stagnation of the 1930s. The process of disruption was repeated by the Second World War. Crucial and still-existing institutions were created during and after the Second World War, for example, the World Bank and the International Monetary Fund (IMF). The victorious powers also managed to establish international trade cooperation, meant to stimulate economic growth. And of course, the Bretton Woods agreement introduced the application of Keynesian economics.

Bretton Woods was designed to regulate the economic and financial system. When necessary, state power would be exercised. State power, indeed, was the distinctive aspect of the Keynesian economics it adopted. This was not limited to "interference"; regulations were thought essential to govern market activities. It should be noted that the success of Keynesian economics, which lasted until the early 1980s, was not significantly affected by the Cold War.

There were various reasons for the failure of Bretton Woods and Keynesian economics. In the early 1970s, after decades of annual growth rates, economic growth and relative success began to decline. The prices of natural resources—especially fuel prices—caused remarkable shortcomings in the economic system worldwide. Inflation, recession, and stagflation were not simply concerns but facts—as they are today—with oil importers suffering more than others. While developed economies recovered quickly, emerging economies had to take on huge amounts of debt that hampered their economies into the 1980s. Personally, I remember Turkey's participation in the Eurovision Song Contest with the famous singer Ajda Pekkan. The title of the song she sang was dramatic: "Oil!" She won twelve points from Morocco. It was a good match: the two countries shared Islamic values; moreover, Morocco exported oil and Turkey imported it.

The outcome was the collapse of Bretton Woods and the end of Keynesian economics, which favored state involvement when and if necessary. The dream of the free market returned under the name of neoliberalism. Above, we observed that Marx began his economic analysis on the basis of free-market conditions, in which buyers and sellers freely meet in the marketplace. Neoliberalism, above all else, is merely the new guise of a no-rules approach in defiance of regulation. For neoliberals, regulation constitutes only an impediment and barriers that restrict their use of capital to accumulate more. This is, to me, exactly how Marx defined credit money. Recall that he said that credit money wants to be free of any type of commitments, boundaries, and the like. What would Marx tell us if he were to see Wall Street?

It is not my intention to explore the collapse of the Soviet Union in detail in this context; however, after the two major failures of the socialist bloc—the 1968 events and, especially, the collapse of the Soviet Union itself—neoliberalism acquired an almost unstoppable momentum. The Soviet collapse not only discouraged socialist movements but also had a social and even psychological impact, suggesting to many the eternal eclipse of socialism. Thus, the 1990s witnessed the transition of the former Soviet Union and other socialist states to so-called freedom and the free market. The United States, largely benefiting from this development, enjoyed robust growth that was also fueled by tremendous advances in information technology.

These advances were interrupted first by the dot-com crisis and then, most notably, by the subprime-mortgage crisis that gave rise to the Great Recession of 2007–2009.[52] It is very interesting to see how mainstream economists explain the latter. They link the financial crisis to 9/11 and the US military adventures in Afghanistan and Iraq. The following paragraph is indicative of the way that a financial crisis, in part caused by an unregulated market, is treated by these economists:

> Soon into the first decade of the twenty-first century, the industrial economies slowed down. The shock of the terrorist attacks on September 11, 2001 turned the attention of the United States to homeland security. The US launched incursions into Afghanistan and Iraq. And toward the end of the decade, the US economy fell into a deep recession, prompted by a financial crisis that originated in the overextended housing market. Other high-income economies with similar excessive spending and financial recklessness also suffered sharp downturns. Unemployment rates soared and government budget deficits mushroomed. The sovereign debt problems of some of the weaker economies in the European Union, particularly Greece, not only threatened the nations of the euro zone, but cast a pall over the entire international financial system, significantly hindering the recoveries of the industrial economies. The developing economies too experienced slowdowns in their growth, in large part due to the reduced international trade. Progress in reducing extreme poverty was hampered.[53]

As we see, the text suddenly jumps from the incursions in Afghanistan and Iraq jumps to the financial crisis. What is the link between these facts? How could they be linked to one another? This we cannot see in the text. It is an abstraction. In fact, some military actions were ongoing until the occurrence of or before the financial crisis. However, it does not explain the whole story. But if I argue that the United States wanted to preserve—and extend—its geographical control while aiming to produce capital beyond—or say, without—production with the help of its unregulated financial system, it starts telling me a story which I find realistic.

What is important for the progress of Sustainable Finance is a thoroughly regulated financial system. Not only should that be a system that sets out regulations in terms of liquidity and capital adequacy ratios, but it should also set concise principles and timelines for the transformation and implementation of 2050 net zero targets.

History is an essential tool that helps us see paradigm shifts. Neoliberalism made most of us live in the now. To live in the now, to live the moment; these are also neoliberal paradigms that we hear almost every day from life coaches and gurus; however, when we look at the historical facts, we can easily find statements exactly made under the same topic and quite the opposite at different times. Regulation versus deregulation is no exception. Before the Paris Agreement, and in the hegemonic expansion of neoliberal politics, it was not unusual to see how deregulation was praised:

> In the power sector, for example, the main innovations have been in terms of deregulation and the introduction of competition through independent power producers (IPPs). Deregulation has allowed energy prices to be gradually freed to reflect the full cost of supply. The energy utilities have begun to access domestic and foreign capital markets by demonstrating to investors acceptable financial practices and competitive returns. However, the new financing mechanisms for the power sector are not without problems with regard to environmental sustainability. The financial incentives to investors favour conventional thermal power, and low energy prices for consumers (as a result of competition) favour increased energy consumption.[54]

Lin See-Yan indeed represents deregulation as a great innovation. The above passage is very striking, one has to admit, but it also gives rise to misgivings. Deregulation allows free entry to the power sector—*by whom?* Competition, another major innovation (!), is exercised by independent—*rhetoric!*—power producers. Pursuant to these innovations, utility firms are able to enter foreign and domestic capital markets, where they can lure investors to fund their projects with attractive prices—attractive for credit money, to be sure. However, and unfortunately, even though financing depends on all these attractions and entertainments, environmental sustainability is nowhere to be found. Incentives increase the use of thermal energy and consumers use more energy. Consumers are always to blame; if they use, they use too much; if they refrain, they should use more. But someone should look at the precious investors: they have money, and thus social power.

Regulation is a requirement. Nonetheless, we still must question whether regulations are enough to meet net zero targets and whether net zero targets are realistic. What would credit money do when faced with barriers (as we have seen, and as Marx reminds us, it despises barriers)?

The answers to these questions touch the reality behind appearances. Then the truth that lies behind the fine rhetoric becomes visible to us. We can continue our inquiry with an examination of financialization.

Financialization and Its Potential Impact on Sustainable Finance

Above, I stated that financialization deserves its own dedicated section. Financialization, for me, represents the expansion of capital beyond the production process. Financialization is the phenomenon that reveals that capital has penetrated every aspect of our lives and made us into successful or bad financial officers.

Financialization is a term generally employed by Marxist economists. Recently it has received particular attention from John Bellamy Foster[55] and Costas Lapavitsas.[56] Others have increasingly studied the phenomenon, perhaps not as thoroughly, but work on the topic is ongoing. Malcolm Sawyer observes that there are two main (Marxist) camps holding different definitions of financialization: the first emphasizes the increasing role of finance through the evolution of the financial sector, while the second claims that capitalism entered a new stage through financialization, and that changing its form changed.[57] On the other hand, Foster cites Robert Pollin as giving special credit to Harry Magdoff[58] and Paul Sweezy[59] as having pioneered in first pointing out what financialization means, that is, the expanding role of finance within the capitalist economy. Although there is no consensus on the term, for me, financialization principally represents capital money that grows beyond the real economy (industrial capital). Most of the scholars and researchers cited above agree on the historical fact that financialization became ascendant in the early 1980s, at the same time as the rise and dominance of neoliberalism. Its expansion and growth were fed by ever-proliferating types of financial products—options, derivatives, futures, asset-backed securities (including the mortgage-based securities that played a major role in the financial turmoil of 2007–2009). Financialization designates what might be called the "gambling era" in the history of capitalism. Far removed from industrial capital, it helps the owners of finance capital to accumulate more money capital without sullying themselves with the dirt of production! The financial sector has expanded into such a giant industry that it now offers an immense range of products whose characteristics are not well understood even by those issuing them; they are rather in the hands of so-called quants, who develop myriads of new products based on financial engineering. The film *Rogue Trader*,[60] based on the book by Niam Leeson,[61] does an excellent job of showing how an investment banking broker brought Barings Banks—one of the biggest banks in the United Kingdom—to bankruptcy by investing in products that escaped internal audit. By the time his disastrous gambling was discovered, bankruptcy was inevitable. This event was a warning, at the global level, that such products constituted a major threat to industry and to common people.

However, no one took adequate measures, and the issue had a much more calamitous impact during the 2007–2009 financial turmoil. The outcome is that finance is no longer a "dynamic factor in accumulation instead becoming a dead weight on the social reproduction process as a whole."[62]

In the third volume of Marx's *Capital*, we see that interest-bearing capital and credit systems become independent in the circulation and accumulation of capital. The tension between industrial capital and money capital, whatever the capitalist form, ends in the tendency to accumulate capital from capital itself. Industrial capital operates on a real basis, whereas money capital creates money—as capital—without production. This tendency of money capital, and what we now call financialization, represents the immanent evolution of this aspect of capital, in which money capital's self-accumulation is propulsive, and even unstoppable, with no resistance from industrial capital, regulators, or the general public.

Addressing the immanent relation between money and state power, Harvey observes:

> But we may now have arrived at the point where the "immanent relation" between money and the state has become so tightly bound that it is impossible to imagine a state power that can regulate and control financialization from the outside. Evidence for this can be seen in the recent Dodd-Frank financial regulatory reform act in the United States, which was basically written by bankers and, to the degree that its implementation was left vague, is being undermined clause by clause largely according to the desires of the banking lobby. But if I am right about the long-lasting role of the state-finance nexus in the history of capitalism, then this "immanence" goes back to the origins of capital itself.[63]

What Harvey says is true and supported by an important historical fact that took place after the 2007–2009 financial crisis. Whether or not to regulate financial markets is a task that belongs to the state or to bodies appointed by the state. The state is not a power removed from finance—or industrial—capital. On the contrary, it consists of the owners of capital and their representatives. There is a complex internal struggle between money capital and industrial capital, but no decisive split between them. Industrial capitalists may struggle against the dominance of finance capital, but with the rise of neoliberal craze, they also form a part of financialization. Anything else would be a misunderstanding of how financial markets work. Industrial capitalists, including their multinational corporations, engage with finance capital to a great extent. To run its business, a firm needs financial capital. To raise financial capital, it is common practice for firms to issue debt securities such as corporate bonds, preferred stocks, collateralized debt obligations (CDOs), and collateralized mortgage obligations (CMOs). The last two contributed to the great financial harm that led to the financial turmoil of 2007–2009. Another common practice is to issue and sell common stocks. How much debt and how much equity a firm has reveals the capital structure of a firm. More debt normally means more risk. Conversely, more equity usually means lower risk. The debt-equity ratio may indicate the risk status of a firm. Over and above its other functions, corporate finance promotes a firm's robust capital structure. How it structures capital signifies how a corporation finances—and targets—its operations and growth.

Capital structuring might mean debt, as just outlined. A firm may issue preferred stocks or bonds. To calculate a firm's financial leverage, one needs to look at the overall capital structure of the firm. The more stocks or bonds issued, the higher its leverage. The question, then, is: why leverage the firm instead of taking credit as direct debt? One reason is the so-called tax shield made possible by the United States' Corporate Income Tax Law. A tax shield may allow a firm to deduct some expenses from its taxable income. However, it may also be the case that the company would gain more benefit from the issuance of bonds or preferred stocks than it would from direct indebtedness to financial institutions. For instance, if a firm issues a corporate bond at a 5 percent fixed interest rate, and if banks offer the same firm credit at 7 percent, the company will choose to issue bonds rather than contract debt with a bank. It is not surprising that former bankers become corporate managers, structuring their new employers' capital. But this is rather simplistic. There is a positive aspect, as former bankers also help companies structure their capital robustly and optimally. Certainly, this is what a textbook on corporate finance might state. This is another abstract-concrete issue, and, as always, the truth lies behind the appearance.

We may now have a better idea of how financial leverage can give a firm more possibilities. More debt means that a firm has greater financial capacity—of course, it is also indebted and has to repay the debt. The risk is greater as well; if a firm does not have sufficient income, it will not be able to benefit from the above-noted tax shield, and leverage will reduce the firm's equity and overall value. External capital has two apparent sides: increase of external debt and return versus externally held capital. In simple terms, if a company has a 10 percent return on its investment, and if it can normally sell 100 units of goods with its own capital, it will be able to generate 100 x 10 percent = 10 units as a benefit. If, instead, the company increases its finance capital by issuing bonds and is able to sell 300 units of goods, its income will increase to 300 x 10 percent = 30 units. Such is the risk-reward of financial leverage.

With the rise of financialization, it is more common for firms to finance themselves or to use intermediaries such as investment banks. The commissions they pay to financial institutions benefit from competition. Only high-risk firms or start-ups pay higher rates of interest and commissions to finance agents. I have simplified this structure, as this is not a finance study, but it is important to infer realistic assumptions from these financial processes. In a world of capital where growth is the essential factor, we can understand that firms inevitably adopt leveraging as the dominant financial management tool. Their intention is to avail themselves of externally provided financial capital and then produce more products to sell at a profit. This system is not sustainable, although the proponents of sustainability claim that strategic growth can be done reasonably and sustainably. These are abstract claims that will never be concrete.

Empirical evidence shows that the retail industry, groceries, and utility companies use financial leverage to a great extent. Indeed, their excessive use of financial leverage might open the gate to bankruptcy. And, talking about "gate," airlines also largely rely on financial leveraging. Trans World Alliance—although its bankruptcy was not due to financial leveraging alone—is an example of how airlines can go bankrupt amid fierce competition and financial leveraging. Concrete, empirical events are the best case studies to test abstract terms like "reasonable," "sustainable growth," and so on. The most striking one of all was perhaps the collapse of Lehman Brothers and others in 2008. Their success was based on the derivatives and financial leverage they used; their failure was due to the same financial products.

David Harvey's extensive work on Marx's *Capital* provides striking information that helps us understand the nature of financialization and how it derives and posits itself as an opponent to industrial capital. Harvey provides a very illuminating and revealing example. He observes that banks can both provide working capital loans to property developers and give consumers mortgage-backed loans that enable them to buy the properties the developers build.[64] However, Harvey argues that there is not the same amount of demand for the two types of loans.[65] In the first place, if there is a possibility for the creditors to benefit from easy and cheap credit, they could easily create an investment bubble financing both sides. Second, we find that capital controls not only production, but exerts remarkable control over the consumer side as well. Financialization, therefore, impacts both macro- and microeconomics.[66] In fact, rising profits accrued through such financial transactions gain weight and have no need for any relation to surplus value—meaning, that is, that they are free of industrial capital. This is what Costas Lapavitsas calls "financial expropriation,"[67] which changes the social and financial aspects of society.

If the impact of financialization is so very great, then the question inevitably arises: how does financialization relate to Sustainable Finance? This question is vital. It provokes one to wonder whether Sustainable Finance is the negation of the current financial system or just another form of it. This deserves a logical and convincing answer. The proponents of Sustainable Finance might argue that regulation is coming back into the financial world. However, this answer is rather immediate and thus abstract in the Hegelian sense. What if financialization intends to absorb Sustainable Finance as it emerges into the history of the capitalist system? In fact, simply arguing that Sustainable Finance represents the negation of deregulation may be illusory, and we need a better understanding to grasp what is going on in the domain of finance.

The point to be determined is whether capitalism has entered a new era. This is hard to say. We might look at this from another perspective: as an oscillation—or, rather, a struggle—between financial capital and industrial capital. This might help us gain a better understanding of what is going on around us. I was curious about the status of finance versus production. As we know, financialization is stronger in the Anglo-American world, in the United States and the United Kingdom, for instance. I took a quick look first at the economic indices of the United States and China, where I assumed production still dominated—everybody uses Chinese goods. I was not wrong: I discovered that the service industry is much larger in the United States, while China's production is much higher than that of the United States. Logically, this indicates that the US economy suffers from a double shortfall in competition with China: labor power and production derived from this labor power. As a consequence, the United States would expand financialization based on accumulated capital in order to compete with China. Such was my first reflection on the topic. I then scanned some literature and found further support. My point is that the United States has lost the production battle against China, most probably permanently, and the only chance it has is to push growth based on financialization at the expense of people in a hopeless struggle against the Chinese type of capitalism—and this includes the option of war.

What it is important for us to know is that financialization, inevitably, targets nature. Not only will nature be destroyed by its business-as-usual processes; the finance industry will also be directly involved in its exploitation. Beyond the extravagant programs, summits, and declarations, this appears to be the next major development in today's financial reality. Using Ajl's terms, we could argue that the "financialization of nature"[68] will be one of the new struggles between eco-socialists and capitalists:

> capitalism destroys in order to create. The foreclosure of some fields of investment means prising open others. For the burgeoning "Great Transition," several arenas are key. First, infrastructure, enfolding the gargantuan electricity and power sectors—the core of industrialization, and a central arena of interest for the Wall Street Consensus. Second, perhaps much more ominous, is the reboot of wrecked REDD and REDD+ agendas. The acronym stands for reducing the emissions from deforestation and forest degradation. The + adds in conserving stocks of forest carbon, sustainable forest management, and the enhancement of stocks of forest carbon. However, these programs often wove deciduous woodlands and tropical rainforests into the price nexus, financializing nature through carbon markets which put a price tag on "eco-system services."[69]

Nature as capital may not be an old concept. In a brilliant article, Foster blames COP26 for opening the gates to the "expropriation of the earth."[70] Foster's remarkable analysis makes it clear that net zero targets and the concept of natural capital accord with each other and allow finance capital to treat our planet as a simple object of exploitation. Adjusting carbon emission quantities through trading is just the solution that such capitalists would propose—but a capitalist solution is no solution. Sustainability is the mask that conceals this disastrous fact for and from many who claim they want a green planet.

Summary and Conclusion

Paradigms are one of capitalism's greatest illusions. The fight against climate change is itself a nice paradigm; however, the truth behind the paradigm is that the capitalist economy continues to control society, nations, and nature. Rhetoric gives rise to new paradigms, but it repeats the same flow (a flow of paradigms—not actions) without a concrete outcome. In previous chapters, we saw how the UN set targets in the 1990s and 2000s for 2005 and 2020; today we hear the same rhetoric for 2030 and 2050—and, in the case of China, for 2060. Capitalism conceals facts behind abstract universality.

Net zero by 2050 is a very good fairy tale, but impossible to achieve given the current targets, practices, and regulatory framework. As long as it remains of secondary (if not lower) importance to profitability and growth, sustainability is merely another paradigm keeping "one-dimensional man" (Herbert Marcuse) and society under control. Capitalism also works in reverse; it calls for a sustainable planet but hides practices that undermine sustainability. In relation to sustainability, profitability and growth cannot be omitted; these concepts constitute the core of the capitalist economy, and they should be dealt with appropriately.

Achieving net zero carbon emissions may seem like a positive step in tackling climate change. However, some argue that the concept suffers from several flaws and limitations. It has no bearing on historical emissions. It does not address the fact that many countries and companies have contributed to the problem with decades of high emissions. It places a disproportionate burden on developing countries, which are expected to reduce emissions substantially, although developed countries are not called to account for their historical contributions. Reliance on unproven technologies, such as carbon capture and carbon storage, which may not be commercially available or economically viable in the near future, will likely be required to achieve net zero carbon emissions. Relying on such technologies could induce a false sense of security and delay the adoption of more immediate and effective measures to reduce emissions. It can lead to carbon offsets and greenwashing. Companies and countries could use carbon offsets, such as planting trees or investing in renewable energy in other countries, to compensate for their own emissions. But this can be problematic as it may not result in a net reduction of emissions and can instill a false sense of achievement, or greenwashing. It has no regard for social and economic factors. Achieving net zero carbon emissions may require significant changes to current economic and social systems, which may have unintended consequences, such as job losses or a rise in inequality. Social and economic problems could arise from focusing exclusively on reducing carbon emissions without considering broader impacts. In short, net zero is part of capitalist abstract universality.

Deregulation and regulation are two sides of the same coin. When we talk about deregulation and regulation, we are talking about the structure of financial markets and the regulations that govern them. This is another aspect of capitalist realism. It prevents us from talking about the object itself; instead, it tells us how it is going to be treated—in this case, by the financial markets. In principle, the problem is not with the regulation or deregulation of financial markets; the problem lies in the structuring of finance capital and the markets themselves. After the collapse of Bretton Woods and the relatively stable growth of the imperialist economies, the 1970s saw the emergence of a real struggle in the world economy. It was the end of Keynesianism, and the gates were thrown open to the advocates of neoliberal economics. It was a time when the non-intervention of the state in financial markets was celebrated; only remember Michel Foucault's false statements about neoliberalism and his historically unjustified claims about governmentality. As expected, the illusory solution was the promotion of neoliberal economics, which intended the annihilation of state intervention and financial regulation—that is, deregulated markets. This paradigm caused the explosion of financialization, which has since invaded the world economy.

As previously explained, deregulation does not mean unregulated financial markets. On the contrary, it implies *re*-regulation which, thanks to the regulatory bodies, gives the market the power of self-regulation. To argue that deregulation means more regulation is not perverse. Deregulated markets, the neoliberal economy, and financialization are all linked; they are all signs of the nature of finance capital, which hates any control that prevents it from accumulating without limits.

Financialization represents an authoritarian power that subsumes everything—the universal subsumes the particular, which loses all difference in identity. It abolishes all particulars and desires to become One; this One abolishes all differences without reserve. We can think of this in terms of the theory of the state in the Hegelian system. For Hegel, a true state is one that ensures that particulars exist under the universal. The historical and logical analysis of capital, on the other hand, shows us that financialized capitalization exploits the working class and establishes its dominion over productive capital. Reason tells us that this will radiate as a singular and authoritarian power if the situation does not change.

Faced with financialization, this analysis of the singular can only be reversed (abolished) by abolishing financialization and the system that gives rise to financialization. For this reason, a thorough program to develop methods of resistance needs to be put in place. This is not a problem that can be solved in the mind alone. A transformative practice is required. No decisive steps can be taken to achieve sustainability for the planet and its inhabitants unless the exploitation of people and nature is abolished.

Sustainable Finance is not sustainability for the benefit of human beings. It is another phase and "converted form"[71] of global capitalism in decay, although proponents of capitalism promote it as a sustainable way to achieve profitability and growth. I conclude that capitalism should be negated, succeeded by another system; one that provides a transition and a new, Marxian direction.

Notes

1 McKinsey, "What is Net Zero?," *McKinsey*, November 28, 2022, https://www.mckinsey.com/featured-insights/mckinsey-explainers/what-is-net-zero.

2 IPCC, AR6, Climate Change 2022: Mitigation of Climate Change. Working Group III contribution to the Sixth Assessment Report of the Intergovernmental Panel on Climate Change (Intergovernmental Panel on Climate Change, 2022), https://www.ipcc.ch/report/ar6/wg3/downloads/report/IPCC_AR6_WGIII_FullReport.pdf

3 For details, I would encourage the reader to read through the IPCC AR6 directly. 500 $GtCO_2$ is not the only budget defined; it stems from the historical emissions and probabilities about the future. Thus, it would be useful to note that 500 Gt is about 1.5 degrees of global warming with a 50 percent probability. As a comparison, if the probability is set at 67 percent, the global budget goes down to only 400 Gt. 500 Gt is the so-called market practice, and I take it as the reference, although it is not the only projection. Perhaps there is no need to mention it, but there are uncertainties to a large extent.

4 IEA, "CO_2 emissions in 2023," *IEA*, March 2024, https://www.iea.org/reports/co2-emissions-in-2023.
5 Holly Jean Buck, *Ending Fossil Fuels: Why Net Zero is Not Enough* (London: Verso, 2021), 30–4.
6 Ibid., 30.
7 Vera Eckert and Tom Sims, "Energy Crisis Fuels Coal Comeback in Germany," *Reuters*, December 16, 2022, https://www.reuters.com/markets/commodities/energy-crisis-fuels-coal-comeback-germany-2022-12-16/.
8 CNBC, "Germany's Increased Coal, Oil Use will be Temporary, Scholz Says," *CNBC*, July 16, 2022, https://www.cnbc.com/2022/07/16/germanys-increased-coal-oil-use-will-be-temporary-scholz-says.html.
9 Ibid.
10 Rob Schmitz, "Amid an Energy Crisis, Germany Turns to the World's Dirtiest Fossil Fuel," *NPR*, September 27, 2022, https://www.npr.org/2022/09/27/1124448463/germany-coal-energy-crisis.
11 Jessica Dillinger, "The Top 10 Coal Producers Worldwide," *WorldAtlas*, June 14, 2020, https://www.worldatlas.com/articles/the-top-10-coal-producers-worldwide.html.
12 Reuters, "Britain to Keep Coal-fired Power Plants Open this Winter," *Reuters*, July 29, 2022, https://www.reuters.com/business/energy/britain-keep-coal-fired-power-plants-open-this-winter-2022-07-29/.
13 Deutsche Welle, "Germany Commits €100 billion to Defense Spending," *Deutsche Welle*, February 27, 2022, https://www.dw.com/en/germany-commits-100-billion-to-defense-spending/a-60933724.
14 Ben Knight, "Where is Germany's Military Budget Going?" *Deutsche Welle*, March 18, 2022, https://www.dw.com/en/german-military-big-budget-little-efficiency/a-61136184.
15 Karl Mathiesen and Zia Weise, "Greta Thunberg calls Germany Using Coal over Nuclear a 'Bad Idea,'" *Politico*, October 11, 2022, https://www.politico.eu/article/greta-thunberg-germany-using-coal-over-nuclear-bad-idea/.
16 Ibid.
17 James Dyke, Robert Watson, and Wolfgang Knorr, "Climate Scientists: Concept of Net Zero is a Dangerous Trap," *The Conversation*, April 22, 2021, https://theconversation.com/climate-scientists-concept-of-net-zero-is-a-dangerous-trap-157368.
18 Bonnie Waring, "There Aren't Enough Trees in the World to Offset Society's Carbon Emissions—and there never will be," *The Conversation*, April 23, 2021,

https://theconversation.com/there-arent-enough-trees-in-the-world-to-offset-societys-carbon-emissions-and-there-never-will-be-158181.

19 Georg Friedrich Wilhelm Hegel, *The Philosophy of Mind*, trans. William Wallace and Arnold V. Miller (Oxford: Oxford University Press, 2007), 5.

20 The Network for Greening the Financial System, About us https://www.ngfs.net/ngfs-scenarios-portal/about.

21 Ibid., https://www.ngfs.net/ngfs-scenarios-portal/explore.

22 McKinsey, "What is Net Zero?".

23 In this study, I use "CO_2" and "carbon" interchangeably, in line with usage in the relevant literature.

24 McKinsey, "What is Net Zero?".

25 Ibid.

26 Max Ajl, *A People's Green New Deal* (London: Pluto Press, 2021), 52.

27 Ibid.

28 Ibid., 53.

29 Brett Wilkins, "Climate Scientists: 'Net Zero' is a Dangerous Trap," *Climate and Capitalism*, April 22, 2021, https://climateandcapitalism.com/2021/04/22/climate-scientists-net-zero-is-a-dangerous-trap/.

30 Bloomberg, "ESG May Surpass $41 Trillion Assets in 2022, But Not Without Challenges, Finds Bloomberg Intelligence," *Bloomberg*, January 24, 2022, https://www.bloomberg.com/company/press/esg-may-surpass-41-trillion-assets-in-2022-but-not-without-challenges-finds-bloomberg-intelligence/.

31 Earthsight, "Flåtpacked Förests: IKEA's Illegal Timber Problem and the Flawed Green Label Behind it," https://www.earthsight.org.uk/flatpackedforests-en.

32 See e.g., CSRHUB, IKEA Group ESG Ranking, according to which IKEA has a score of 94 (80–100 is the highest range), https://www.csrhub.com/CSR_and_sustainability_information/IKEA-Group.

33 Akepa, "Greenwashing: 11 Recent Stand-Out Examples," *Akepa*, July 23, 2021, https://thesustainableagency.com/blog/greenwashing-examples/#ikea. This website contains other important examples and information about sustainability.

34 Ibid.

35 Sustainalytics, "Company ESG Risks: The Coca-Cola Co.," https://www.sustainalytics.com/esg-rating/the-coca-cola-co/1007904888.

36 European Environment Agency, Climate and Energy in the EU, Transport, Real World Emissions, EEA, n.d., https://climate-energy.eea.europa.eu/topics/transport/real-world-emissions/intro. I recommend the readers to look at the datahub of the EEA, where one can find a vast number of data points that would

solidify the understanding of actions and mitigations taken toward climate change, together with their impacts.

37 These figures are taken from https://www.worldometer.com/coronavirus.

38 Andreas Schrimpf, Hyun Song Shin, and Vladyslav Sushko, "Leverage and Margin Spirals in Fixed Income Markets during the Covid-19 Crisis," Bank for International Settlements, Bulletin No. 2, April 2, 2020, https://www.bis.org/publ/bisbull02.htm.

39 Mathias S. Kruttli, Phillip J. Monin, Lubomir Petrasek, and Sumudu W. Watugala, "Hedge Fund Treasury Trading and Funding Fragility: Evidence from the Covid-19 Crisis," Finance and Economics Discussion Series 2021-038 (Washington: Board of Governors of the Federal Reserve System), https://doi.org/10.17016/FEDS.2021.038.

40 UNEPFI, "Testing the Application of the EU Taxonomy to Core Banking Products: High Level Recommendations," https://www.unepfi.org/industries/banking/eu-taxonomy-testing-core-banking-products/.

41 UNEPFI, "Turning the Tide: How to Finance a Sustainable Ocean Recovery," https://www.unepfi.org/publications/turning-the-tide/.

42 UNEPFI, "Guidelines for Climate Target Setting for Banks," https://www.unepfi.org/publications/guidelines-for-climate-target-setting-for-banks/.

43 UNEPFI, "A Legal Framework for Impact: Sustainability Impact in Investor Decision-making," https://www.unepfi.org/publications/a-legal-framework-for-impact-sustainability-impact-in-investor-decision-making/.

44 Jeffrey Sachs, *The End of Poverty: Economic Possibilities for Our Time* (London: Penguin, 2005), 42.

45 See Ian Angus, *Facing the Anthropocene: Fossil Capitalism and the Crisis of the Earth System* (New York: Monthly Review Press, 2016), 35.

46 CDP, "Finance Sector's Funded Emissions over 700 Times Greater than its Own," https://www.cdp.net/en/articles/media/finance-sectors-funded-emissions-over-700-times-greater-than-its-own.

47 NZBA, "Our Members," https://www.unepfi.org/net-zero-banking/members/.

48 IEA, "Steel," https://www.iea.org/energy-system/industry/steel.

49 IEA, "CO2 Emissions in 2023: Emissions Grew in 2023, but Clean Energy is Limiting the Growth," https://www.iea.org/reports/co2-emissions-in-2023/emissions-grew-in-2023-but-clean-energy-is-limiting-the-growth.

50 IEA, "CO2 Emissions in 2023: Coal Demand in Emerging Market and Developing Economies was the Biggest Driver in Global Emissions Growth," https://www.iea.org/reports/co2-emissions-in-2023/coal-demand-in-emerging

-market-and-developing-economies-was-the-biggest-driver-in-global-emissions-growth.

51 Jean Baudrillard, *Simulacra and Simulation* (Michigan: The University of Michigan Press, 1994), 19.

52 I used the Great Recession of 2007–2009 and the 2008 crisis interchangeably.

53 Peter N. Hess, *Economic Growth and Sustainable Development* (New York: Routledge, 2013), 5.

54 Lin See-Yan, "Chairman's Summary and Recommendations," in *Finance for Sustainable Development: Testing New Policy Approaches*, ed. Juergen Holst, Donald Lee, and Eric Olson (New York: United Nations, 2002), 26–7.

55 John Bellamy Foster, "The Financialization of Capitalism," *Monthly Review*, April 1, 2007, https://monthlyreview.org/2007/04/01/the-financialization-of-capitalism/.

56 Costas Lapavitsas, "Theorizing Financialization," *Work, Employment and Society* 25, no. 4 (2011): 611–26.

57 Malcolm Sawyer, "What is Financialization?," *International Journal of Political Economy* 42, no. 4 (Winter 2013–14): 5–18.

58 Robert Pollin, "The Man Who Explained Empire: Remembering Harry Magdoff," *CounterPunch*, January 6, 2006, as cited in John Bellamy Foster, "The Financialization of Capitalism."

59 Robert Pollin, "Remembering Paul Sweezy: 'He was an Amazingly Great Man,'" *Counterpunch*, March 6–7, 2004, as cited in John Bellamy Foster, "The Financialization of Capitalism."

60 *Rogue Trader*, directed by James Dearden, 1999.

61 Niam Leeson, *Rogue Trader: How I Brought Down Barings Bank and Shook the Financial World* (Boston: Little, Brown & Company, 1996).

62 Cédric Durand, *Fictitious Capital: How Finance Is Appropriating Our Future*, trans. David Broder (London: Verso, 2017), 191.

63 David Harvey, *A Companion to Marx's Capital: The Complete Edition* (London: Verso, 2018), 577.

64 Ibid., 590.

65 Ibid.

66 Thomas I. Palley. "Financialization: What It Is and Why It Matters." Washington: Levy Economics Institute of Bard College, *Working Paper No. 525*, December 2007, 1–31.

67 Costas Lapavitsas, *Profiting Without Producing: How Finance Exploits Us All* (London and New York: Verso Books, 2013), 376.

68 Max Ajl, *A People's Green New Deal*, 89.

69 Ibid., 40–1.

70 John Bellamy Foster, "Nature as a Mode of Accumulation," *Monthly Review*, March 1, 2022.

71 Converted form is an important concept that I take from Merab Mamardashvili. Drawing upon Marx, Mamardashvili describes the inner workings of complex systems and how they become hidden and concealed because of their appearance. Sustainability and sustainable development (and Sustainable Finance, too) are good examples of converted forms since their outward manifestations appear as a distinct entity that is self-adequate, independent, and a just path for the combat against climate change. Merab Mamardashvili, "Converted Forms: On the Need for Irrational Expressions," *Stasis* 5 (2017): 204–17.

5

How to Achieve Better Sustainability?

A Philosophical Discourse

In order to open the Marxian framework in a new way, I propose a systematization that includes the disciplines of biopsychology and social psychology in relation to the philosophical field. Before presenting the details of this proposal, I wish to state that this does not involve any call to cancel any part of the Marxian framework. On the contrary, it aims to import new insights at societal and individual levels. My principal argument for the necessity of social psychology is based on the requirement to revisit the concept of collective social consciousness and memory. Similarly, I argue that we need to revisit the concept of the individual in society. The social aspect has readily been accepted as key to understanding the Marxian framework. However, the individual level is often omitted or even scorned. My argument is that the individual level was not omitted or scorned by Marx himself; however, he and Engels did not dedicate any studies to this topic. Thinkers in their tradition, on the other hand, have tried to employ and integrate the category of the individual: Adorno, Horkheimer, Marcuse, and Fromm, thinkers who either belonged to or had some association with the Frankfurt School. In their work, the individual is interpreted in largely psychoanalytical terms, a "method" that has continued into our own day. We are familiar with the influence of Lacan on French intellectuals and on the famous philosopher Slavoj Žižek. In my proposal, psychoanalysis would continue to play a part; however, the social sciences and psychology would contribute even more to philosophy and the critical theory of society. Both social psychology and biopsychology, although still relatively new fields, provide valuable information about and insights into society and individuals, including us. An engagement with social psychology and biopsychology would require a long-term project. In this chapter, I confine myself to drawing a framework that demonstrates how they can interact with philosophy and how philosophy can benefit from these fields.

Since I coined the term "biopsychopolitics," in this study, I will discuss biopolitics and psychopolitics because of their evident etymological relation. Another reason for my discussion is my critical approach to the thinkers most famous for deploying biopolitics and psychopolitics, Michel Foucault and Byung-Chul Han. Today, criticism of Marxism is routine and commonplace. It is nevertheless an interesting irony to encounter people who seize every opportunity to declare that Marxism is over yet persist in dealing with something they dismiss as antiquated. The end of the era of grand narratives was a positive advent. However, it is significant that the currents of thought developed in their place, which have themselves become paradigms, have made almost no progress, failing even to create an agenda. This is why I also discuss and criticize Foucault's biopolitics and Han's psychopolitics.

I now move on to biopsychopolitics and the space it occupies within the Marxian framework. It is important to stress again that biopsychopolitics is neither a revision of the Marxian framework nor itself an all-encompassing framework. On the contrary, it is an orientation and ground for social and individual analysis and for the interrelation between the individual and society.

Biopsychopolitics

Biopsychology "is the scientific study of the biology of behavior."[1] It is the scientific domain, a subdiscipline of psychology, that studies "physiological, evolutionary, and developmental mechanisms of behavior and experience."[2] Biopsychology—also called psychobiology, biological psychology, behavioral neuroscience,[3] physiological psychology—addresses the central nervous system and is thus closer to neuroscience than to biology. In my view, it is a domain that philosophers should study as well, since it involves the mind-body problem, epigenetics, and other similar concerns that would assist critical thinking.

Drawing on biopsychology, a part of psychology considered as a social science, I propose biopsychopolitics. This is a new domain, one that studies the impact of the central nervous system on behavior and psychology. I coined this term to illuminate how the biological domain causes behavioral outputs in the domain of finance. In connecting biology and behavior, my purpose is to transcend Foucault's governmentality-based biological approach as well as to explain the shortcomings of Byung-Chul Han's psychopolitics, which he presents as almost the antithesis of biopolitics. In other words, although the term I propose draws on Foucault's and Han's concepts, its content is radically different.

In terms of finance, the central nervous system is constituted by the rules and apparatus of the capitalist system and the state. Financial regulations and frameworks oppressively condition society and the individual. A biologically conditioned society and individuals develop adaptive or reactive behaviors in relation to the system. This is where I engage with biopsychology to articulate the societal and individual problems that were a great concern in the last century and that continue to occupy us. One of the philosophers whom I have found most inspiring, Herbert Marcuse, deals with human psychology in masterpieces such as *Eros and Civilization* and *One-Dimensional Man*; however, my claim is that, today, biopsychology affords philosophers and critical thinkers with more comprehensive materials, as these can be employed to look at society and the individual in terms of the organism. Besides, biopsychology (a) emphasizes the unity of the body and mind and (b) offers scientific findings about the impact of biology on human behavior and psychology.

Foucault's Biopolitics

Foucault introduced the concept of biopolitics in his lectures at the Collège de France, first in 1975–6[4] and further elaborated in 1977–78[5] and 1978–79.[6] His lectures on the birth of biopower actually focus on several topics: governmentality, liberalism, neoliberalism, and the like. In the twelve lectures, we expect Foucault first to introduce particular topics and then elaborate on biopower in the later lectures. However, since he spent so much time on the topics as just mentioned, this was not possible.

In one of its aspects, Foucault's philosophical framework is the negation of Althusserian-type structuralist Marxism. Althusser, without seeming to feel the need for proof, claims that the mature Marx distanced himself from Hegel—this constituted an epistemological break. While I do not wish to examine this proposal in detail, even a cursory reading of the *Grundrisse* and *Capital* (the first volume, especially) suffices to refute Althusser's distinction between a young and a mature Marx. On the contrary, Marx seems to admire the logical structure of the Hegelian system and, as we demonstrated in Chapter 2, largely applies it in the *Grundrisse*. For his part, Foucault seems to have difficulties with Marxism's ideological and structural interpretations. Instead, he proposes a genealogical framework served by an archeological method.[7]

In our own day, the control Foucault identifies has grown even stronger: the more digitalized we are, the more controlled we are. In every macro- and microsystem, we see the apparatus of control at work. When we use electricity, when we are on vacation, when we consume unusual amounts of energy sources—all can be easily controlled through surveillance and monitoring. If we use a specific political language or discuss certain topics—art, music, health, and so on—this is easily and effectively monitored, providing a perfect opportunity for cookie sellers like Facebook and Google to provide us with meticulously tailor-made advertisements.

In brief terms, which admittedly fall short of a full characterization, Foucault studies the transformation of the art—his word—of governing in history. When he talks about biopower, he attributes it to the evolution of a population toward a new structure and concept. For Foucault, political economy took the place of law in the eighteenth century. Law required the external intervention of the state, whereas political economy operated internally. Political economy arises from the fact that the state should limit its activity. For Foucault, this constitutes a major shift in the model of governmentality, the emergence of a new rationality that allows phenomena to flow by themselves—laissez-faire. Foucault maintains that when we talk about liberalism, we need to understand this type of governmentality as connected to truth based on this new practice of self-limitation. For Foucault, liberalism is necessary to grasp the concept of biopolitics.

Throughout his lectures, Foucault informs his audience of the evolution of governmental approaches from discipline and punishment to liberalism, each succeeding state representing itself as a rational opposition to previous stances on government. For Foucault, there are principally two reasons for the effort to think outside of Marxian categories. First of all, Foucault claims to go beyond Marx—a fair claim. Second, Foucault observes that the communist bloc failed to provide freedom in their own societies—another fair claim.

That the claims are fair is not to say that the analyses are correct. Proving an argument false does not guarantee the truth of all the counterarguments. Yet this is where Foucault invested much of his thinking. However, his methodology, partly inherited by Deleuze, did not inspire further work for more than a few decades and even then, without any remarkable practical engagement or outcome. As this chapter deals with sustainability and biopsychopolitics, I cannot provide a lengthy critique of Foucault's writings. Nonetheless, it is important to notice that, while claiming to go beyond Marx, he falls—anachronistically—next to Marx, as he dismisses any transformative powers or sees them elsewhere. I cannot say whether he does this deliberately, as part of his mission, or simply because he cannot grasp the role of economics, but his lengthy survey changes the flow of historical facts. For Foucault, for instance, the shift from mercantilism to physiocracy was rather an alteration in thought and the art of governance. On several occasions, he mentions technological advances and urban transformation, but neglects to emphasize the role of changes in productive modes as determinative for thought. He treats governmentality as an isolated art of governance but fails to provide sufficient evidence to relate its shifts to developments that have neither a relational nor causal character.

For me, Foucault is the perfect exemplar of a researcher who deepens a given field. He is very good at articulating details and providing a wealth of information about the archaeology of knowledge, as well as histories of sexuality, the prison, mental illness, etc. On the basis of these developments, he characterizes what Marx and Marxists, like Althusser, said about the state as mechanistic and deterministic. Such accusations, as we all know, continue to be very popular today. Yet, whatever he says about determinism and mechanistic approaches, etc., Foucault himself does not bring anything to light. This might appear to contradict my earlier statements about his contributions to knowledge. But there is no discrepancy. When we gather his writings together, we can see that he justifies Marx in his findings and thinking. I will explain and then leave the topic for now.

Imagine that our topic is football. I make the general statement that if both teams in a match play offensively, the audience enjoys the spectacle, as there will be more goals. I then provide some examples from past World Cup games or national leagues. My interlocutor interrupts and says, "But in a game between England and Germany, although both played offensively, the final score was 0-0." This does not refute my claim but fairly and justifiably provides an exception. Foucault generally plays the role of this interlocutor. He provides details, and more details, and even more details, but, to a great extent, the result still justifies Marx's historical materialist view of state power, the transformation of the modes of production, and more besides. The situation is rather like Engels's *The Dialectics of Nature*. Most of what he said in that work was valid in terms of the science of the time, but no longer valid today since many of its claims have been falsified. Some would still fault him for writing about Kant's and Laplace's theories. But Engels's methodology and proposals remain largely valid even today, and this is not difficult to see. In this spirit, I sometimes refer to Foucault on a particular topic, but the benefit of his writings is mainly complementary to another, principal category—for example, economy and mercantilist history.

Foucault maintains that sovereign power was mainly based on the right to kill. Neoliberalism is the negation of this type of power, defending free competition and installing a regressive juridical power. With this transformation, Foucault argues, the law becomes more normative, and the new technology of power focuses on life, not on murder.[8]

Nothing that his analyses are focused on Western societies, Foucault represents biopower and biopolitics as arts of governing that focus on life, noting that punishment, discipline, and biopower can all coexist. Perhaps unconsciously, Foucault thus provides a typical example of Hegelian sublation (*Aufhebung*). What he treats as developments in governmentality are no doubt examples of Hegel's preservation-in-cancellation. Even in biopower's focus on life (*bio*), Foucault does not deny that the right to kill may still be preserved. Nonetheless, this preservation justifies itself through scientific knowledge instead of belief. Without explicit reference, Foucault is here referring to Western epistemology's link to justified belief. On the other hand, his emphasis on rationality is unjustified in most cases, since he neglects the disguise of rationalization. The scientific justifications proffered when Nazis massacred Jews did not represent true scientific knowledge; this was mere barbarism based—only if necessary—on pseudoscience. There was no rationality in the conduct of the killers, only the exercise of rationalization. Reason and rationality can only criticize and condemn such barbarism.

Foucault's ambiguous language and vague explanations caused confusion among scholars. Their conclusions are based on their own views of Foucault.

His defenders extended his interpretations while his detractors criticized views that could be interpreted otherwise. For my part, when I adopt a historical perspective, I see Foucault gradually distancing himself from Marxism. This remote attitude mainly derived from his hatred of Soviet Marxism, including the French Communist Party, but extended also to Marx and the whole Marxian tradition. There is nothing wrong with this stance; the error lies in Foucault's interpretation of facts. For example, equating the scientific knowledge employed by German Nazism with the overall framework of scientific knowledge is illusory and confusing. To defend his construction of power and governmentality, Foucault dismisses the oscillation between democracy and fascism, even utterly rejecting the more robust analyses undertaken in his lifetime. His aim was to defend the "*bio*" function of the so-called new governmentality at all costs, forcing him to disdain important facts that he synthetically tried to overcome. Such an approach includes two layers that are in contradiction with each other. On the one hand, it presents new knowledge about generally ignored or dismissed facts; on the other hand, it negates all other interpretations based on the state, democracy, and power. To overcome this situation, a negation of Foucault (a negation of the negation) followed by the employment of new concepts is necessary, although this is not the main aim of this study.

Foucault's analyses of liberalism and neoliberalism are no different. He provides a wealth of information and knowledge about these systems and their governmentalities. Foucault's analyses employ a historical approach that negates previous modes of power and knowledge. As it is pertinent to this study, Foucault's assessment of neoliberalism deserves special focus. Foucault discusses neoliberalism in his 1978–9 lectures. He addresses the governmentality and rationality of neoliberalism that, for him, divides into two categories: the German neoliberalism that emerged from the so-called Ordoliberals, and the American neoliberalism rooted in the Chicago School.

Foucault's construction rests on two pillars: he criticizes Nazism as a failure of liberalism but praises neoliberalism for its postwar reconstruction of Germany. The Chicago School, for its part, shares the same stance as Foucault: their common enemy is the state. Although they differ in the details of their theoretical perspectives, the state that both varieties of neoliberalism oppose is the state that exerts control over the economy.

What Foucault is unable to perceive is the illusory aspect of neoliberalism. He views neoliberal governmentality as the vehicle of a productive subjectivity that tolerates different identities, choices, preferences, and the like, and thus in opposition to disciplinary governmentality in its essence. In his eighth lecture, Foucault suddenly deviates into French social and political issues. This was at the end of the 1970s, when neoliberalism was expanding its reign globally. That is, France was just starting to adopt a neoliberal economy and polity as Foucault gave his lectures. For Foucault, neoliberal economics and politics serve to overthrow the remnants of socialism. In his view, poverty and other social issues could not be remedied by socialism; neoliberalism offered a solution. Was Foucault unaware of Margaret Thatcher's TINA (there is no alternative)? Was he wholly ignorant of miners' strikes in the United Kingdom? His aversion to talk of state-imposed repression apparently blinded him to what was coming. It seems that repressed social classes did not aim to provide a toolbox to defend society. Averse to the Nazi and Stalinist state, as though they were equivalent, Foucault claims that only the state-phobic can fail to see the ongoing reduction of state power. Foucault was never able to grasp that socialism pertains to society and not the state. For this reason, the state and its apparatuses could easily be replaced by other organs. In criticizing those who criticize the notion of the state, Foucault misses the basic point: what creates the state? Today, nation-states are back on the scene, and, arguably, they are stronger than ever. Foucault almost completely misses the dialectics of economy and politics due to his wrong starting point.

For Foucault, neoliberalism can motivate emancipation from disciplinary sovereignty.[9] Foucault's atomic, individualistic, subject-oriented approach, thus, describes the neoliberal subject as a self-interested rational being capable of conducting an analysis of the social domain that will provide rational outcomes and results. This subject does this to foster its own position in the competitive environment of social life. But this is simply a defense of the current societal dispensation that is not far distant from capitalist realism. Foucault's position, at best, allows for a critique of society that, in extreme cases, would result in some reforms. For Foucault, a radical social transformation does not appear necessary; some ameliorations in neoliberal governmentality would render more rational beings. Foucault regarded and promoted neoliberalism as a form of governmentality that can be both oppositional and governing. He does not consider neoliberal governmentality as the antithesis of the state. From the opposite angle, however, the same statements could be made for any polity that today supports Keynesian economics for its opposition to deregulated markets.

Foucault's intention is not to provide a criticism of capitalism or Marxism, as the categories he develops are not fit for such a purpose. On the contrary, his analyses of neoliberalism depict secure competition that ensures the preservation of the free market, transforming the moral and political environment of society and the individual as well. Individuals (or "subjects" in his terminology), accepting this competitive order, act properly and learn how to make strategic choices and calculations, undertaking and making use of calibrated investments. Foucault should perhaps have written an economics textbook. It might have proved one of the most popular in the current education system. Foucault goes on to praise the way individuals settled in such a system through their multiplicity, learning to entangle life in its diverse aspects, and so on. As Gabriel Rockhill observes, Foucault constructed a system not unlike Ptolemy's model of the universe with the Earth at its center.[10] The same problem afflicts Foucault: the categories have a wealth of content and teem with historical facts, but the categories themselves (in themselves) are erroneous.

We do not know whether Foucault undertook these analyses for a specific purpose. We are not mind readers. We cannot advance an accusation without clear evidence. Nevertheless, we do know one thing about Foucault: he distanced himself from Marxism more and more, especially after the failure of 1968. His hatred of and despair about Marxism seems to have forced him, like other French anti-Marxists, to develop a new framework based on a completely different mode of social and individual analysis, one with its own genealogy. Indeed, according to Foucault's lectures, the historical flow of neoliberalism began in the 1930s, with the German Ordoliberals. Yet it is revealing that Foucault chose to praise neoliberal governmentality at the end of the 1970s, when the world was entering a new type of capitalism, one that welcomed financialization and deregulation (as I have observed and explained in this study). In 1979, when Foucault was giving his lectures, the detrimental character of neoliberalism, being indoctrinated everywhere, was clear to see. It is hard to believe that a thinker of his caliber disregarded the events in Chile, where neoliberal government had come into force, let alone the changes in the United States and the United Kingdom. As should by now be evident, neoliberalism and its economic policies have since taken over our everyday lives, at the expense of the working classes. On the most generous reading, Foucault's praise of this kind of governmentality could be regarded as a significant failure on the part of a thinker many claim to be radical. In fact, for me, Foucault is an advocate of the neoliberal system, one who fought against Marxism and the transformation of society.

Foucault, who strangely enough calls Marcuse a pseudo-Marxist, claims that the state is not simply oppressive (as explained above). For Foucault, the new form of governmentality does not produce a uniform, standardized "one-dimensional man," in Marcuse's words. On the contrary, it encourages multiplicity, free choice, rational calculation: we are all entrepreneurs, competitors in a free market. Foucault's analysis ends where Marx's begins, with the myth of the free market. He completely misses the point and promotes illusory phenomena as evidence of the success of neoliberal governmentality—this is exactly what capitalist governments want to do!

Foucault's ontology is as irrational as his approach to subjectivity. Neoliberal governmentality does not truly offer a free market; it only allows the owners of capital to make us believe, through their illustrious success stories, that by becoming entrepreneurs in a free market, we can be one of them. Beyond the philosophical deficiency of this view, we see another defect of the Foucauldian framework: it cannot offer a solution for ecological catastrophe. The destruction of nature clearly accelerated after the 1970s, and the reason for this is the insatiable character of finance capital and financialization. To praise neoliberal governmentality is simply to contribute to those crimes from the perspective of philosophy. To confront neoliberalism means negating Foucault's false arguments about it.

Byung-Chul Han's Psychopolitics

Byung-Chul Han introduces the concept of psychopolitics.[11] The book in which it appears is not very long. Mostly, it is a collection of aphorisms held aloft by rhetoric. Indeed, its content is rather limited despite the apparent claim of going beyond Foucault's biopolitics.

Han is not wrong, though he does not grasp the whole picture. He is not able to tie psychology and biology properly and behaves as though these two faculties are separate. In fact, they are linked, and psychology is, to a great extent, if not in all aspects, the outcome of biological factors.

Han states today's capitalism "is fundamentally different from nineteenth-century capitalism, which operated by means of disciplinary constraints and prohibitions."[12] This is true, but it is both a fact and an appearance. Han does not discuss the historical process of capitalism. With the exception of a few who insist on the same facts dogmatically, all, including the proponents of capitalism, would promote changing capitalism and capitalist society. The important point is the cause and relations of change. Disciplinary constraints and prohibitions are less visible on the surface; this is true. But analysis should go beyond appearance.

Han distinguishes psychopolitics from biopower (biopolitics):

> disciplinary power does not focus on the psyche. The *orthopaedic* technology of disciplinary power is too crude to penetrate into the deeper layers of the soul—with its hidden wishes, needs and desires—and take it over. Bentham's Big Brother only observes inmates from the outside. His panopticon is bound to the *optical medium*. It has *no access to inner thoughts or needs*.[13]

For me, it is a mistake to separate *psyche* from *bio*. Disciplinary power operates on psyche through biological and disciplinary tools. Yet Han insists on isolating psychology, which cannot exist without biological causes. It is like claiming that thoughts can exist without a brain that receives stimuli from the external world. Even if the brain works—sometimes—without external stimulus, its processes are still based on what previously gathered and stored stimulus. Han created a psychological world from which biology is omitted. His work would be much more useful if he had discussed the psychological outcomes of biological factors.

For Han, Foucault is the main point of reference—as evident even in the title of his work. He proposes an escape from neoliberalism by referring to Foucault's proposal of an "art of living" and "experience":

> the art of living, as the praxis of freedom, must proceed by way of de-psychologization. This serves to disarm psychopolitics, which is a means of effecting submission. When the subject is de-psychologized —indeed, de-voided (*ent-leert*)—it opens onto a mode of existence that still has no name: an unwritten future.[14]

In other words, one should escape into an open—unwritten—future by means of "depsychologization." I do not know if Han has "decolonization" in his mind, but his proposal sounds as weak as some of the concepts of decolonization. Above all, such ambiguous rhetoric does not greatly assist the emancipation of society and individuals. Once psychology is separated from biology, escape is reduced to the depsychologization of the subject. Simply put, before even a proper treatment of depsychologization, it is obvious that subject and society need to abolish the biological support that produces psychological effects. Han's work is inadequate because of this separation and its ambiguous proposals. This atomistic approach that addresses the function and role of the particular is the new trend, popular even among critics of capitalism, and this makes us wonder how it is possible to confront neoliberalism when its methods and means have been internalized. The greater whole is nearly always missed by such approaches: the subject is rather like a drowning person talking about a ship that is sinking.

This is why I employ the term "biopsychopolitics." Although the term requires a much broader definition and framework, I will limit its use to its connection to the financial system. That is, I will not be able to present biopsychopolitics in all its aspects. But this is not my aim, as I see it as the dynamic basis for future research and development. Thus, I limit myself first to drawing up its framework and methodology, and then relate the framework to Sustainable Finance.

How to Employ Biopsychopolitics

Foucault challenged—though gradually, as mentioned above—the Marxist conception of power. Not only did he target Marxism as such, but also the efforts, by Herbert Marcuse among others, that aimed to introduce a biological and psychological dimension into the Marxist framework.[15] Marcuse's draws inspiration from Freud and the latter's repression theory. For Marcuse, life is a struggle between Eros and Thanatos, the pleasure principle, and the death drive. Foucault rejected this model for its overemphasis on repression. For him, power and the state were not merely agents of repression. On the contrary, the state cares for the life of its citizens, seeks to make them live longer, educates them, etc. Interestingly, Foucault's defense is almost like that of a proponent of capitalism. His fake radicalism gradually starts to defend and then advocate neoliberalism. Ironically, he promoted neoliberalism in the years that our planet was growing much more vulnerable to the devastating impacts of neoliberal politics and economics.

The major defeats of the left in 1968 and 1991 gave rise to a new type of intellectual, one who sought to identify irreparable gaps and shortcomings in socialist theory and Marxism. Some, like Ernesto Laclau and Chantal Mouffe, tried to transcend Marxism through radical democracy—future to the back; others seemed to replace demands with desires, like Slavoj Žižek and Alain Badiou. A common point of all these radical thinkers is the reduction of revolutionary and transformative demands to desire. They all promote subjective desire while distancing themselves from social transformation. And yet they claim to be leftists. My point is that their views are based on a misconception of the Marxian framework.[16]

Biopsychopolitics has two principal components: the first is the central nervous system that receives stimuli from the external world: the state, society, other individuals, and nature. The second is the internal connections on which the psyche operates. Biopsychopolitics, thus, represents an individual who is subject to the external world, but whose internal world works on this interaction. This is the biopsychopolitics of the individual. On this layer, cognitive science and cognitive psychology would be companions of this philosophical framework, along with social psychology.

The broader sense of biopsychopolitics lies at the societal level, which forms the second layer. Here, the concern is the formation of society in its relations to what is "above" and "below" (e.g., society against the impositions of the state or governmentality; the impact of society on its individual members). This sphere would be closely connected to the social sciences, particularly sociology and social psychology.

Whatever the validity of his psychoanalytic claims, Freud's attempt to revive the role of the unconscious in our daily lives was courageous. His emphasis on the pleasure principle and the death drive is still important in our individual and social relationships. My aim, however, is not to imitate the Frankfurt School in this respect and merely incorporate Freud or psychoanalysis into a philosophical framework. Rather, my goal is to build on the spirit of the Frankfurt School while using a different framework to transform society toward a better future. For instance, my main difference from Marcuse can perhaps be summarized simply: where Marcuse applies Freudian repression at a societal level, I maintain that the web of relations between society and the individual can be better comprehended if we philosophize about the findings of social psychology.

Biopsychopolitics should focus on the following major points:

(a) The impact of society on the individual—social psychology
(b) The impact of the individual on the self through the central nervous system—biopsychology operating with cognitive psychology when applicable.

These two points should be treated interconnectedly. They are not isolated from one another; on the contrary, they impact each other. The main difference between the two was long ago stated by Marx in "The Eighteenth Brumaire of Louis Bonaparte":

> Men make their own history, but they do not make it just as they please; they do not make it under circumstances chosen by themselves, but under circumstances directly encountered, given and transmitted from the past. The tradition of all the dead generations weighs like a nightmare on the brain of the living.[17]

Marx grasped the essence of the nature of society. He speaks of the transformative agency of society and individuals while remaining aware of the impact of structures inherited from the past, which still rule, guide, and direct society and individuals. That is, their essential aspects did not change, but their forms developed and changed throughout history. Awakening from the nightmare means transforming society and individuals such that horrors are minimized or, in the best case, abolished. What Marx brought to light was that institutions form society and individuals; however, individuals and society—viewed from the collective perspective—can also transform structures. This requires the negation of the current status quo by perception and consciousness gained through praxis.

Applicability of Biopsychopolitics

I discussed the inherent limits and shortcomings of capitalism in Chapter 4. Some questions remain: how can we achieve sustainability and a sustainable financial system? how can we transform society if transformation is even possible? Undoubtedly, these are questions that require book-length studies to construct a critical theory of society. They would include both social criticism and a theoretical framework for transformation. Nevertheless, some essential premises can be offered here.

It is important to remember that the answers proposed are not definitive. They are possible and plausible but subject to continuous reshaping and revision in constantly changing social conditions. Herein lies the difference between a truly scientific approach and orthodox Marxism. Orthodox Marxists are of the opinion that socialism and communism are inevitable, even if it is true that we cannot predict when these forms of society will materialize. However, we know from scientific evidence that any such materialization is easy to avoid. I once had a discussion in which my interlocutor said to me, "It is scientific. The experiment happened in 1917." To which I replied, "But, in 1991, we all saw that the experiment failed." The main problem with any kind of deterministic approach is that it leads to a passive messianism, in which people wait for the revolution to come. One should not ignore the basic reality that transformations are possible. But this does not guarantee that they will be realized. In fact, Marx and Engels mentioned, "Communism is for us not a state of affairs which is to be established, an ideal to which reality [will] have to adjust itself."[18] Our task, therefore, is to provide a sharp criticism of the present structure of society and then to develop and propose a theoretical framework for its transformation. In doing so, we have to keep in mind the nature and purpose of the empirical sciences. Hegel insists on the presence of thinking in the empirical sciences.[19] For him, these sciences aim to develop universal principles, an effort that belongs to their very essence.[20] However, their activity is based on "what is present"[21] and this is the inessential.[22] This indeed was one of the major problems with positivism; however, this obstinacy faded with the coming of the cognitive revolution. Second, and building upon this, philosophy can benefit from the discoveries and development of the empirical sciences, as long as it is aware that they are subject to change. Invoking Hegel again, we can say that philosophy (or what Hegel calls "speculative science") does not turn away from the empirical sciences; on the contrary, it takes them into consideration but employs them for philosophy's own categories.[23]

My own experience—based on practice and many discussions—tells me that a single crucial factor is mainly responsible for the possible shortcomings and even fallacies of an analysis of society: disregarding the difference between the natural sciences and the social sciences. Their essential difference needs to be stressed, even though this work does not deal specifically with the philosophy of science and its methodology. I once had a friend who identified himself as a Marxist. He was knowledgeable. He had an academic background and was cultured, but during our many discussions, he very directly compared social and natural phenomena. I will never forget his giving the example of two molecules of hydrogen and one of oxygen; this is water. He then went on to base a social analysis on this chemical formula. No useful analysis of society can be made by taking such a positivist approach. The main reason for this is that it completely ignores the human factor, in fact reducing the human being to an inorganic substance.

Social phenomena and social sciences require greater elaboration than the natural sciences can provide. If we have the necessary tools and knowledge, we can—under normal circumstances—predict when an asteroid will pass by the Earth, or when the next solar eclipse will take place. However, I cannot know whether or not I am going to be angry this evening, or what will happen in the country next year. Human beings and society are constituted of a myriad of variables that, in the present state of our knowledge, no computer system or human mind can analyze in an efficient way. If we knew what would happen in a country in a year's time, we would all become rich (materially speaking). In *The German Ideology*, Marx and Engels draw a sharp distinction between the natural and the social sciences.[24] In order to provide better predictions, big data, artificial intelligence, and machine learning are used to analyze existing data trends, behaviors, and such. However, the success rate is still too low—well below the fantasies concocted about these developments. We still need our minds, which are not (yet) replaceable, and we should use them as well as possible.

How can we deal with the uncertainties that characterize the behavior of human beings and society? What is their role in society and the human psyche, and what would their role be in the transformation of society? Are the proposals and frameworks currently on offer sufficient to provide adequate answers and realize possibilities? The alternative to the capitalist system is socialism. This is mainly based on abolishing private property and ensuring the collective ownership of the means of production. However, lacking a solid theoretical framework, socialism no longer has many adherents. Accepting this situation is a crucial step on the road to a better society. Indeed, one needs to start from the fact that socialism, as applied or attempted, has suffered several defeats. The most important defeats occurred in the spring of 1968 and in the 1991 collapse of the Soviet Union. Proposing an ideological framework attuned to scientific developments, while stressing the difference between science and ideology, is another crucial step. This is a difficult problem, but one that needs to be addressed. Otherwise, ideological failures are inevitable—and ideology, by its nature, is prone to failure. I will now discuss some basic aspects of the relation. This is a high-level overview and is not meant to be comprehensive.

The Ownership of the Social Means of Production—Discrimination

The ownership of the social means of production has been a matter of concern for centuries. In Marx's framework, the means of production should be the property of society. In other words, the private ownership of property should be abolished. Marxists are not the only ones who hold this position; anarchists and social ecologists, to a great extent, agree. Although these groups criticize each other, their goal is the same: a society without classes and without oppression. I am not saying this to reconcile the ideologies that advocate the abolition of private property. My point is simply to show that among those who claim to oppose capitalism, one of the shared tenets is the abolition of private property.

What can ownership tell us? In our own era, and also historically, we know that the majority of people do not own the means of production. They work for those who do and receive a wage. Thus, at a highly abstract level, we have the owners of the means of production and those who do not. One of the main reasons for this division is discrimination. People from poorer families are more likely not to own the means of production. What can social psychology tell us about this situation? Many things, based on empirical evidence: economic and social inequality, problems regarding access to education, basic material goods, work-life balance, and a host of others. Observation demonstrates the self-justification of the superior group. Generally, the wealthy or the elite regard themselves as meriting their position. Social psychology tells us that our observation is true: the superior group justifies itself by emphasizing the inferiority of the Other.[25] We notice how justification relates to discrimination. How do the oppressed react to this justification? Some would rationalize the attitude and accept it, whereas others would find it intolerable and resist. We can make a further inquiry into how the oppressed act when confronted with discrimination. Here again, social psychology and biopsychology would help us with our philosophical investigation. For instance, justification is a mechanism that the superior party uses to avoid questioning its own status, even whether the superior party's own conduct causes inequality and discrimination.[26] Such information, enriched by narratives and further examination, can provide valuable information about oppression.

Class Consciousness and Inequality

One of the major components of Marxism is class consciousness. This consciousness is the driving force that leads the working class to transform society by revolution. An unavoidable fact is that, in the past, this consciousness failed to realize much, especially during the years of revolutionary struggle against Western capitalism, for example, in Germany and Austria. Revolutions failed; more tragically, a significant segment of the working class supported authoritarian, even fascist movements and regimes.[27]

Today, it is generally admitted that the concept of class consciousness was largely overlooked by the field of social psychology.[28] Indeed, the concept of false consciousness, upon which György Lukács built his work on class consciousness, contains a psychological dimension. For these reasons, it is detrimental to isolate class struggle from the field of psychology, and for philosophy not to avail itself of the findings of psychology. Richard Wilkinson and Kate Pickett state that those who are prey to inequality develop lower interpersonal trust levels.[29] Lukács considered this inequality the basis of class consciousness, the potential ground for the transformation of society. Class consciousness has several consequences for the oppressed: in gaining class consciousness and struggling to change society, it is very likely that the oppressed would face a variety of dangers[30] such as criminalization, imprisonment, and so on. What is noteworthy is that, among other things, class consciousness is caused by inequality, itself another form of discrimination. And this discrimination is intrinsic to capitalism, which deprives many people of the ownership of the means of production and divides society into classes.

Other concepts are eligible for similar reconsideration: alienation, reification, and so on. Social psychology and biopsychology can provide valuable insights for philosophy. They may also help us to better understand our research object and avoid possible biases.

Now that I have examined a couple of examples of the application of biopsychopolitics and showed how it can treat such concepts in the field of philosophy, I will proceed to points that would play a role in the transformation of society.

Class-Related Issues

The capitalist economy is prone to crises. These crises occur due to the immanent problems already examined in this study. Economists and the proponents of capitalism propose solutions that oscillate between regulation and deregulation. No one identifies who is doing the regulating or deregulating. All of them, by accident or design, conceal the real reason: the ownership of capital, which is the result of the mode of production. We are aware that the accumulation of capital causes social injustice. Among its other social effects, it creates various types of discrimination against the poor, the uneducated, and the disadvantaged. This makes it obvious that any better outcome in the capitalist system is a myth: the system itself will always be vulnerable to crises. What remains hidden is the ever-present class struggle in its various forms.

To be effective in fighting climate change, the opposition forces need to embrace two main facts: the first is that the climate struggle is linked to and forms part of the class struggle. In the last few decades, there has been a growing acceptance of this view, but orthodox Marxism still tends to see the climate struggle—as well as the feminist struggle and the lesbian, gay, bisexual, transgender, queer/questioning, plus (others) (LGBTQ+) struggle—as complementary to the struggle of the working class. Domenico Losurdo[31] and Matthew T. Huber[32] have written at length on this subject. When discussing the oppressive nature of capitalist society, we cannot deny that capitalism exploits nature and discriminates against women, LGBTQ+, and other groups. Instead of resisting these facts and ever-changing conditions, we need to rethink how to define class struggle today in a way that includes the oppressed—and nature—under the same umbrella.

Such a reconsideration of the notion of class struggle is not necessarily "revisionist" in the Leninist sense of the term. However, one should remember that Lenin himself was one of the twentieth century's most notable revisionists. The way he used the dictatorship of the party was itself the greatest single revision of Marxism. Therefore, we should first consider what class struggle meant in Marx's time and what it means in ours. This would enable us to draw a distinction, if necessary, between social structures and the relevant concepts. Concepts change over time for a simple reason: their conditions and reality change. The concepts of anthropology, psychology, phenomenology, and many other disciplines change over time. It would be absurd to declare that change occurs elsewhere, but that the components of the class struggle and the classes themselves have remained the same.

For Marx and Engels, the class struggle was a struggle that culminated in the antagonism between the bourgeoisie and the proletariat.[33] Nowadays, many people strongly criticize this notion for various reasons. Some object that history is not the history of class struggle, that we should see "history as a struggle of ideologies and quest for justice,"[34] while others claim that class struggle is no longer at work. While I admit that the "classical" struggle was mainly between the working class and the bourgeoisie, I want to emphasize the historical change in the character of the working class, and also want to draw attention to other emerging facts and classes connected to the class struggle. A new interpretation and understanding of class struggle, and the forms of action based on this new concept, could help transform society. Focusing on the ownership of the means of production and proposing a plan of action can be useful, but it is important to remember that such proposals are subject to an uncertain future and need to be revisited often and revised as necessary.

Social Phenomenology

Western philosophy is concerned with ontology and epistemology. Debates about their relative priority did not last long. However, the most important part of ontology has generally been overlooked. Ontology, the science of being, became the province of the self in its opposition to the other, society. It became even more problematic with Heidegger, who invented a Being, an abstracted form of universality, if I may use Hegelian terminology here. Heidegger felt the damaged life of modern society but sought the answer in illusory restoration attempts. Philosophical thought has mostly set the individual against society or vice versa. In other words, the individual and society have been seen as opposed to each other. We can see this in Hobbes and Freud, for example, where there is no harmony. Being, in this sense, is a being oppressed by society. This conception continues to play an important role in various discussions and worldviews; for example, we see it in the individualism versus collectivism, nature versus nurture, and particularism versus universalism debates, among others. However, all these discussions remain abstract because they look at the phenomenon from a one-sided perspective, one that philosophizes on the basis of the individual.

Badiou is one of Levinas' critics. Although the scope of this work does not include ethics as such, it is still useful to address Badiou's so-called ethics of truth and to consider the main points of his critique. For Badiou, Levinasian ethics is not philosophy, but a "decomposed religion,"[35] theology, and thus, anti-philosophy. For me, it is problematic to set religion and philosophy in complete opposition to each other, at least in terms of their historical development. If something in the Levinasian framework were not on the margins of reason, such a claim would be valid. But accusing another of being irrational, unrealistic, and so on, is not uncommon in philosophy. The essential point to consider is whether the category of the Other fits into ethics. This we can address. Even a Hegelian-Lacanian-Marxian philosopher like Badiou has been a critic of Emmanuel Levinas for the latter's proposal of a beginning with the other. In the Marxian framework, accepting that the individual is a result—also in relation to society—includes, perhaps implicitly, the place of the other. Levinas puts this relationship between individuals first, before examining the relationship to institutions. On the other hand, is this not the moment when Levinas and Adorno meet, when they both emphasize the priority of the Other in their own terms?[36] Non-identity thinking gains more importance here, because any beginning with the subject does not transcend identity thinking, be it the Absolute, or a classless society founded on false grounds. It remains vulnerable to totality and its power exercised on the Other. In other words, I propose reading Levinas from the perspective of negative dialectics. Then, we can better define its problematic parts deriving from phenomenology in general along with the just statements of Badiou about how identities are formed annihilating differences, where Badiou gives a robust example of non-identity thinking.[37]

So how should we think about the social and political dimension of the relations between individuals? Levinas's proposition is sometimes considered impracticable; however, when thoughts are admitted as justified, but not their practicability, we should think twice about the strength of the objection. Whatever is in thought is potentially real. I examined this view—which comes from Hegel—in relation to the transformation of society. I will not repeat the analysis here. However, anything philosophically justified is real and has the capacity for concretization. It is interesting that Marxist thinkers try to close such channels, since their own framework is sharply criticized for exactly the same fault: impracticability. Probably we all know how hard it is to transform ourselves and society, but this does not mean that the pursuit of alternatives is impracticable. There is no guarantee that transformation will take place; it is one of a myriad of possibilities, yet it exists.

I argue that both the contradiction and the harmony between the self and the other play an important role in the Hegelian system. Hegel thought that the age of freedom had arrived, and man would liberate nature and society. We should still keep this as a motto; however, we have to admit that the potential for harm is greater than the potential for liberation. Indeed, Hegel's negative philosophy proposed liberation—freedom—and concrete and absolute unity through negation, but the positive outcome of this process has not yet occurred. Today, after two world wars in the past century, we find ourselves in the midst of economic turmoil, multiplying conflicts, and perhaps even a third world war, which some believe has already begun. History, as the emanation of Spirit in space and time, does not reveal a positive flow that will bring an end to the struggle. In other words, reason does not always materialize as anticipated; it can kill, legislate, and defend such atrocities.

Life is not only fighting and struggle. However, struggle has been inevitable in history. Maria Dimitrova mentions that liberalism and communitarianism are opposed to each other, but both presuppose totality.[38] To relate the individual to other individuals and to society requires a deeper perspective that should not remain abstract. Reconciliation between the self and the other can have a different starting point. Here I refer to Maria Dimitrova and her work on social phenomenology, inspired by Levinas. Sociality is the nature of human interactions and connections, as well as their ethical and political ramifications. In social philosophy, social relations are often treated as an association. This association does not proceed from the state to its members.

It begins with the direct relations of individuals to one another and is thus indirectly linked to other institutions like the community, the state, and so on. Dimitrova claims that this constitutes a rejection of totality, but for her this is not mere rejection. The logic at work differs from the classical variety. In this perspective, intersubjectivity prevails. The multiplicity of relations negates totality and posits our responsibility for the Other.

For Dimitrova, responsibility is the key. When I say "I," every other person is an "other" for me. Dimitrova argues that all negativity stems from this otherness, which presupposes common standards, measures, and so on.[39] This is a lacuna that punctuates one of the central issues in social and political philosophy. It is also one of the fundamental questions in current social and political life. When we encounter a community that seems to live according to different norms, we first attribute a negative otherness to them. We do this on the basis of values that we ascribe to our own community or society. If language is a norm under the flag of a nation-state, we find it bizarre and sometimes even unacceptable for another to speak a different language. The interesting, even sad, fact is that we do not even consider whether those speaking another language settled in the land before us. We speak the official language, and so must they! Even this shows the implicit operation of totality—however monstrous it may become—under the guise of common measures and standards that claim universality. If we want to achieve true universality, in other words, we need to examine the roots of both liberalism and communitarianism.

When we think of Aristotle claiming that justice is the highest virtue, we should not forget the kind of justice that existed in Aristotle's polis. Dimitrova points this out and argues that arguments only make sense if one can first participate in the life of the polis.[40] A system, a regime, a law, is made meaningful through participation. Women and slaves were not included in the polis. This is where I would like to connect the responsibility identified by Levinas and Dimitrova to our social and political life. The issue has persisted throughout history, albeit in different forms. One party—usually wealthier or more educated but, in any case, in power—defines rules for others, claiming that they are universal measures. In one fell swoop, injustice becomes universal justice. How does this happen? It happens because the interpersonal relation between individuals is rejected. In social contracts, ethical considerations, and the like, we see—almost without exception—that first there are predetermined individuals and society, and then rules are provided to govern that society and those individuals. It is an implicit Western trait to conceal the nature of interpersonal relations, affirming that rules, institutions, the so-called virtues, existed before the relations between individuals.

Our current environment and mode of existence are proof that life is not necessarily a process of progressive self-realization; it can experience downturns and setbacks. This makes many people believe that the struggle is endless and that this is the truth of human life. We then think of the other as only a threat to the "I." In the workplace, a skilled person is perceived as a threat to our careers. Such a notion is based on the idea that we "deserve" better conditions than the other. If someone threatens my position at work, my first reaction is to say that I am better educated, speak more languages, possess more technical skills and experience, and so on. We earn and we deserve. This is also one of the main traits of capitalism and neoliberalism. Those who are successful deserve a better life. Those who deserve a better life will rule. They will set the rules and universal policies that others will follow. Ironically, those who deserve to rule will impose rules on those deemed inferior. This is where liberals and communitarians converge, whatever their other differences.

Responsibility is the essential aspect of interpersonal relationships. The other needs our response. This does not mean that the other oppresses me. On the contrary, it is "the primordial need for communication between different individuals."[41] If we do not become aware that both cleaners and doctors, for example, need each other, if we do not feel responsible for the other in such a way that his or her voice is heard, the totality is vulnerable to totalitarianism. This threat operates, as we have seen, in the oscillation between liberalism and fascism, and between the dream of a free classless society and Stalinist dictatorship.

Social and political philosophy should radically rethink its constructs and structures. Thinkers like Kant, Hegel, and Marx accepted the role of interpersonal relationships. However, their arguments were made on the basis of an analysis of property, society, and the state. They did the best they could in their own historical conditions. For example, Marx tried to solve this problem by abolishing private property. However, had he lived after this was attempted, who would deny that he would reconsider the issue from a perspective that included interpersonal relationships? Erich Fromm and Marcuse wanted to bring the individual into Marx's framework. They were almost entirely inspired by a psychoanalytic framework. Interestingly, Marcuse aimed to negate Freud and claimed that oppression was not predetermined. Indeed, although he was not able to fully articulate the view, I believe that Marcuse wanted to reconcile the individual and society; but again, from the angle mentioned above. Before positing the relation between the individual and society, we should first look more deeply into the relations between individuals. Society and institutions follow.

The Other, for Levinas, differs from its earlier treatment by philosophers. The Other is not an other that simply represents a potential threat to me. For Levinas, indeed, communication with the Other is a "fine risk to run."[42] It is a risk because alterity can harm one's ego. Nonetheless, in ethical terms, this is required. It is the Other for whom I am responsible, and the Other's face "is the factor of indomitable resistance to totalization in the system of society and transcends it."[43] Thus, I am for the Other through my responsibility. In that sense, the Other is not plural, nor is it considered as being subject to plurality. If plural, then it ends up as the Third that is no longer a liaison in moral responsibility; it is a matter of social justice through institutions, the state, and the like. As a consequence, the social and political philosophical approach to sustainability and Sustainable Finance should first consider interpersonal relations based on moral responsibility. Instead of seeing individuals as a threat, we should think of how we can achieve a positive outcome based on togetherness. Should we rely solely on rules and regulations? Or should we act responsibly before such rules are elaborated? For example, should we learn from indigenous people how they protected agricultural land, or should we simply ignore them in favor of our own universal measures? The latter policy, even in communist societies like China and the Soviet Union, caused famine. In capitalist society, it continuously causes inequality, poor wealth distribution, poverty, and injustice. To build a better society, we need to think about building human relationships. I do not deny that there should be rules and regulations. At the same time, I believe that private property, the state, and classes should be abolished. But this abolition should not be done directly by law; it should first come from within myself and from my responsibility to the Other. The state, even a stateless society, should only mediate and provide me with channels for my responsibility to the Other. However, I should first become aware of this responsibility and only then join the effort to achieve a stateless society.

How to Form a Line of Resistance Again?

The opposition movements should focus on achieving net zero targets by 2050. However, two types of extremism must be shunned: (a) denying that the targets will ever be achieved and opposing any process; (b) fixing dogmatically to the targets as currently determined. Targets can be determined, but there is never a guarantee of whether they will be met. Robert Pollin is right to find net zero by 2050 realistic, and right when he says that "the core of the global Green New Deal is to advance a global project to hit these IPCC targets."[44] The measure is important. If the capitalist transformation delays or even tries to block the transformation of the political economy, this does not imply that the Left should abandon its goals. Quite the contrary, organizing initiatives to support the transformation, while drawing attention to the failure of the capitalist system to fulfill its obligations, would help justify the Left's efforts and actions. As Kate Aronoff emphasizes,[45] this is not a black-and-white process, and to accept any delay is not an option.

Given the consequences of the collapse of the Soviet Union and so-called real socialism in the early 1990s, we should, without delay, focus on whether and how a transformation into a socialist society is possible. This book is not about the dynamics of such a transformation; instead, it explains that sustainability cannot be achieved through the immanent development of capitalism. Therefore, merely as a proposal, I will conclude this work with some plausible and realistically utopian projections. With "realistically utopian," I refer to the split between utopian and scientific socialism, and also to Herbert Marcuse's utopian framework. For Marcuse, utopia can be realistic. This means that the society we want to achieve is not a mere fairy tale but depicts a reality, one that may not be achieved today but is nevertheless possible. Therefore, it is not necessary to juxtapose utopia and science in the Hegelian manner: the utopia we have does not contradict the possibility of a real world to come. This is a rather complex topic, but a synthesis between utopian and scientific socialism is possible. Rosa Luxemburg observes:

> Far from being a sum of ready-made prescriptions which have only to be applied, the practical realization of socialism as an economic, social and juridical system is something which lies completely hidden in the mists of the future. What we possess in our program is nothing but a few main

> signposts which indicate the general direction in which to look for the necessary measures, and the indications are mainly negative in character at that. Thus we know more or less what we must eliminate at the outset in order to free the road for a socialist economy. But when it comes to the nature of the thousand concrete, practical measures, large and small, necessary to introduce socialist principles into economy, law and all social relationships, there is no key in any socialist party program or textbook. That is not a shortcoming but rather the very thing that makes scientific socialism superior to the utopian varieties.[46]

This statement is still vital to understand socialism and a socialist society. Messianic, orthodox versions of socialism maintained that socialism is simply a set of rules that meets every need. It was a grand theory of salvation. Luxemburg is clearly aware of this tendency and is careful to clarify what socialism is not. Her pronouncement accords perfectly with the progressive approach discussed in our own era. Since human rationality emanates through practice and throughout history, to prescribe what will be done in socialist societies is simply to fall victim to an idealist philosophical approach dominated by ideological deviations. Luxemburg emphasizes the superiority of scientific socialism to its utopian competitors. At first sight, she seems to follow Marx and Engels in rejecting the latter for scientific socialism. Nonetheless, the utopian socialism that she properly and correctly criticizes is not the utopia that Marcuse explores in his writings. It is crucial to grasp this difference. There is a major difference in the sense of "utopia" as used by the utopian socialists and Marcuse. Utopian socialists depict a nonexistent society and concoct multifarious descriptions of how such a society would function. In deep accord with the essence of Marxism, Luxemburg denies this. For Marcuse, however, utopia does not depict what will happen in the future in its smallest details. Utopia signifies rationality and the possibility of a more just future society, and the will to change our existing society into a better one. Thus, Marcuse's utopia aligns with the statements of Marx, Engels, and Luxemburg. Although without quoting or referring to Marcuse, Roy Bhaskar speaks of a "concrete utopianism" very much in Marcuse's sense.[47] We can focus on our utopia to achieve a better society; however, we should not focus on the small details of the latter. We should continue to criticize our current encounters, alert to what we should not carry with us into a better society, just like Luxemburg counsels: we know what we do not want, and what we want to abolish. The rest is the product of our progress and collective praxis. To predetermine the details of a society to come is to make oneself vulnerable to messianic culture. Those who find virtue in depicting the details of a socialist society seem unaware of Marx's own undertaking—the critical analysis of capitalist society and not the blueprint of a socialist one.

The Marxian analytical framework requires the detailed analysis of the society in which we live. Therefore, it is essential to extract the universal part of the Marxian dialectic and to avoid the mere repetition of Marx's political actions, suited to his own era. Who, for instance, would deny that the working class was the motor of a possible revolution when, in nineteenth-century England, 85 percent of the population of London belonged to this class? Today, the working class is still vital for the transformation of society, but its relations to the means of production, the state of its alienation, its life conditions, its weight in society, and many other factors are all different—significantly different. When talking about the proletariat today, we need to revisit the term and take many other societal layers into consideration. We should define the role of minorities, the Other as represented by LGBTQ+, women, oppressed nations, the unemployed as potential workers, and so on. On the other hand, workers who belong to a workplace union (or syndicate) are much less similar to their past counterparts due to neoliberal politics and digital and technological innovations. That is, the analysis of classes is to be done in terms of their relation to capital and their will and ability to bring about transformation. New forms of life require new forms of action and strategy.

For such an organic overview, we need to focus on the oscillation between the maximization of profit and businesses' responsibility to their stakeholders in relation to other determinants. And to do that, we must consider the factors that put pressure on finance capital and check how these factors impact this oscillation. This entails an organic unity, one that encapsulates the dialectical moves of the components within a circle.

Such a task is deeply challenging; yet any proposal would be subject to further empirical analysis by experts in other fields, who would determine whether or not it complies with empirical findings. Here, we will confine ourselves to philosophizing on the basis of the immanent moves of certain units connected to a greater whole. This allows us to consider different alternatives that embrace multiplicities in their relation to the universal.

Take Gilles Deleuze's molecular politics, which I persist in seeing as a potentially alternative mode of thinking and ground for action. Molecular politics' difference from orthodox Marxism has subjected it to general criticism. On the other hand, we should keep in mind that Deleuze and Félix Guattari searched for alternatives following the defeat of 1968. To accept defeat and still try to develop new forms of resistance is itself a virtue. Although I have a number of objections to Deleuze's overall assertions, I believe it necessary to admit the truth, irrespective of its origin. Obviously, no one calls the twentieth century "Deleuzian," as Foucault predicted, but should we not rather focus on the content in pursuit of a better society? When names rather than theory and practice become paradigms, abstract universality and fetishism increase. Thus, I find it fitting to revisit molecular politics and inquire if it contains something for real life.

Movement is imperceptible, according to Deleuze and Guattari.[48] For me, on the contrary, it is rather a problem of the universal and particular in their interrelated becoming. I see every act of resistance to the world system as a movement of the particular against the universal. Every national struggle, LGBTQ+ struggle, fight against climate change, and fight for communal rights and identities is justifiable as a fight against the system, provided that they move both within the system and against it. For instance, acts of environmental resistance oppose the system if they emphasize social inequalities and maintain that social change is required for success against climate change. Similarly, feminism and LGBTQ+ struggles are justified if they are connected to the overall discrimination caused by capitalist economies. National struggles are de facto justified since they counter colonial hegemony. They are even justified and need to be supported if they fail to meet the basic conditions; however, they will be vulnerable to absorption into the world system if they do not draw the lines properly; but, to reiterate, they should be supported in any case. The task of socialists and those opposing the system is not to merely criticize; rather, it is to engage in solidarity for the transformation of society. Think of the Zapatistas in Chiapas or the Kurds in Rojava. They have an autonomous way of life, independent of the nation-state of Mexico in the case of the Zapatistas and Syria in the case of the Kurds. They employ different types of administration, have different worldviews, and so on. However, such particularities stem from their collective resistance: being subject to the oppression exercised by nation-states. Their independent, particular—molecular—form of resistance connects them, perhaps even unconsciously, to other actual or potential movements. They also offer a paradigm: they demonstrate that people can still choose their own way of communal life, even in present conditions. Nation-states are still extremely strong, and such lines of resistance can collapse. But which is better: to wait for a global movement that will save the oppressed or try to win decisions in their own lives?

For me, molecular politics represents a line of resistance, an effort at autonomy that arises from the will and power of regional negations. Such forms of existence should not be underestimated, but neither should they be considered as an alternative to socialism. This is where mistakes sometimes happen. We tend to reject anything that does not fit our beliefs or stereotypes. This is not the scientific or philosophical way, and it also goes against human beings' experiments and developments. The desire that real life accords with our desires is moreover connected to some kind of idealism, the idea that socialism is won by "classic" means: barricades and street battles, or an armed revolutionary struggle from the mountains to the cities, and so on. This is false consciousness and closes itself off from a myriad of forms of resistance. On the contrary, we should embrace the varieties of resistance exercised by people in their own conditions. Their multiplicity-in-becoming composes a symbiosis able to cause the formation—becoming—of other multiplicities that can change the nature[49] of the whole.

Identity-in-difference and difference-in-identity should not be only terms. The universal, in its very universality, should consist of different particulars, and particulars should preserve their own forms within the universal. Otherwise, there is either abstract universality or totalitarianism. A transformation would be possible when the universal and particular are connected to each other in their identity and difference, even as they form a new unity in their becoming. The task of biopsychopolitics would be to reflect upon these lines of resistance in their relation to the whole, concrete universality. Mobilities are likely to differ[50] as they reflect the conditions in which they build their movement; agricultural workers in India and peasants in Latin America develop different forms of resistance, and their differences should be taken seriously and prioritized. On the other hand, where Sustainable Finance is concerned, there is still a tendency to underestimate the role of the fight against climate change and its methods. The old-fashioned view that only a socialist revolution can truly resolve the climate crisis causes only procrastination, and our planet can no longer wait for such a revolution.

Notes

1 John P. J. Pinel and Steven J. Barnes. *Biopsychology*, 11th ed. (London: Pearson, 2022), 28.

2 James W. Kalat, *Biopsychology*, 13th ed. (Boston, MA: Cengage, 2019), 5.

3 Chris Chandler, *Psychobiology* (West Sussex: John Wiley and Sons, 2015), 4.

4 Michel Foucault, *"Society Must be Defended": Lectures at the Collège de France, 1975–1976*, trans. David Macey (London: Picador, 2003).

5 Michel Foucault, *Security, Territory, and Population: Lectures at the Collège de France 1977–1978*, ed. Michel Senellart, trans. Graham Burchell (London: Palgrave, 2007).

6 Michel Foucault, *The Birth of Biopolitics: Lectures at the Collège de France 1978–1979*, ed. Michel Senellart, trans. Graham Burchell (London: Palgrave, 2009).

7 Michel Foucault, "What Is Enlightenment?" [1984], in *The Essential Foucault: Selections from Essential Works of Foucault 1954–1984*, ed. Paul Rabinow and Nikolas Rose (New York and London: The New Press, 2003), 43–57.

8 Michel Foucault, *The History of Sexuality, Volume 1: Introduction*, trans. Robert Hurley (New York: Pantheon Books, 1978), 144.

9 Trent H. Hamann, "Neoliberalism, Governmentality, and Ethics," *Foucault Studies* 6 (February 2009): 37–59, https://doi.org/10.22439/fs.v0i0.2471. See also Jason Read, "A Genealogy of Homo-Economicus: Neoliberalism and the Production of Subjectivity," *Foucault Studies* 6 (February 2009): 25–36, https://doi.org/10.22439/fs.v0i0.2465.

10 Gabriel Rockhill, "Foucault: The Faux Radical," *The Philosophical Salon*, October 12, 2020, https://thephilosophicalsalon.com/foucault-the-faux-radical/.

11 Byung-Chul Han, *Psychopolitics: Neoliberalism and New Technologies of Power*, trans. Erik Butler (London: Verso, 2017).

12 Ibid., 15.

13 Ibid., 20–1; emphasis in original.

14 Ibid., 79.

15 Herbert Marcuse, *Psychoanalysis, Politics, and Utopia: Five Lectures*, ed. Ray Brassier, trans. by Jeremy J. Shapiro and Shierry M. Weber (London: Repeater Books, 2022), 22.

16 Tony McKenna, "Against Post-Marxism: How Post-Marxism Annuls Class-Based Historicism and the Possibility of Revolutionary Praxis," *International Critical Thought* 4 (2014): 142–59. McKenna is very good on Laclau and Mouffe's misconception of Marxian concepts. He is critical of Althusser and Žižek as well. McKenna's discussion of Gramsci is especially relevant, showing how Althusser, Laclau, and Mouffe falsely draw upon Gramsci's works.

17 Karl Marx, *Karl Marx, Frederick Engels: Collected Works, Vol. 11, Marx and Engels: 1851–1853* (London: Lawrence & Wishart, 1983), 103.

18 Karl Marx and Friedrich Engels, *The German Ideology* (Prometheus Books, 1998), 57.

19 Georg Friedrich Wilhelm Hegel, *Lectures on Logic: Berlin, 1831*, trans. Clark Butler (Bloomington and Indianapolis: Indiana University Press, 2008), 24.

20 Hegel, *The Encyclopaedia Logic*, 31 (Explanation to Paragraph 7).

21 Ibid.

22 Hegel, *Lectures on Logic*, 24.

23 Ibid., 33 (Explanation to Paragraph 9).

24 Karl Marx and Friedrich Engels, *The German Ideology*, 34. A crossed-out passage is provided in a footnote: "The history of nature, called natural science, does not concern us here; but we will have to examine the history of men, since almost the whole ideology amounts either to a distorted conception of this history or to a complete abstraction from it."

25 Elliot Aronson, Timothy D. Wilson, and Samuel R. Sommers, *Social Psychology*, 10th ed. (Harlow, Essex: Pearson, 2021), 445.

26 Christian S. Crandall and Amy Eshleman, "A Justification-suppression Model of the Expression and Experience of Prejudice," *Psychological Bulletin* 129, no. 3 (2003): 414–46.

27 Max Horkheimer, *Dawn and Decline: Notes 1926–1931 and 1950–1969*, trans. Michael Shaw (New York: The Seabury Press, 1978). See in particular "The Impotence of the German Working Class," 61–5. Horkheimer draws attention to the situation in which, when employed, the working class does not want change.

28 Hector Carvacho and Belen Alvarez, "Inequality and Class Consciousness," in *The Social Psychology of Inequality*, ed. Jolanda Jetten and Kim Peters (New York: Springer, 2019), 308.

29 Kate Pickett and Richard Wilkinson, *The Spirit Level: Why Equality Is Better for Everyone* (London: Penguin, 2010), as cited in Hector Carvacho and Belen Alvarez, "Inequality and Class Consciousness," 309.

30 M. Carmen Herrera, Francisca Expósito, and Miguel Moya, "Negative Reactions of Men to the Loss of Power in Gender Relations: Lilith vs. Eve," *The European*

Journal of Psychology Applied to Legal Context 4, no. 1 (2012): 17–42, as cited in Hector Carvacho and Belen Alvarez, "Inequality and Class Consciousness," 310.

31 Domenico Losurdo, *Class Struggle: A Political and Philosophical History,* trans. Domenico Losurdo (New York: Palgrave Macmillan, 2016).

32 Matthew T. Huber, *Climate Change as Class War: Building Socialism on a Warming Planet* (London: Verso, 2022).

33 Karl Marx and Friedrich Engels, *The Communist Manifesto*, ed. Frederick L. Bender, trans. Samuel Moore (New York and London: W.W. Norton & Co., 1988).

34 Thomas Piketty, *Capital and Ideology*, trans. Arthur Goldhammer (Cambridge, MA and London: Harvard University Press, 2020), 1035.

35 Alain Badiou, *Ethics: An Essay on the Understanding of Evil* (London: Verso, 2001), 23.

36 Here, I must also credit the work of Eric S. Nelson, who has written a specific work about Adorno and Levinas. From his perspective as well, there is an overlap between these two philosophers in terms of negative dialectics: Eric S. Nelson, *Levinas, Adorno, and the Ethics of the Material Other* (New York: State University of New York Press, 2020).

37 Alain Badiou, *Ethics*, 23–4. Badiou brilliantly discusses how so-called respect for the Other ends up in reality as an imperative that imposes on the Other to become integrated into Western civilization. Thinking about the integration policy of some Western countries, such a brilliant statement is perhaps even more important than the time it was made. However, I cannot see this as a valid critique of the Levinasian framework.

38 Maria Dimitrova, *Sociality and Justice: Toward Social Phenomenology* (Stuttgart: Ibidem, 2016), 14.

39 Ibid., 16.

40 Ibid., 22.

41 Ibid., 23.

42 Emmanuel Levinas, *Otherwise Than Being or Beyond Essence,* trans. Alphonso Lingis (Pittsburgh: Duquesne University Press, 1998), 120.

43 Maria Dimitrova, *Sociality and Justice*, 154.

44 Noam Chomsky and Robert Pollin, *Climate Crisis and the Global Green New Deal* (London: Verso, 2020), 74.

45 Kate Aronoff, "Recharging Internationalism," in *A Planet to Win: Why We Need a Green New Deal,* ed. Kate Aronoff, Alyssa Battistoni, Daniel Aldana Cohen, and Thea Riafrancos (London: Verso, 2019), 120.

46 Rosa Luxemburg, *The Russian Revolution and Leninism or Marxism* (Ann Arbor: University of Michigan Press, 1961), 69–70.
47 Roy Bhaskar, *Enlightened Common Sense: The Philosophy of Critical Realism* (New York: Routledge, 2016), 93.
48 Gilles Deleuze and Félix Guattari, *A Thousand Plateaus: Capitalism and Schizophrenia*, trans. Brian Massumi (Minneapolis and London: University of Minnesota Press, 1987), 280.
49 Ibid., 249.
50 Tim Cresswell, "The Production of Mobilities," *The Cultural Geography Reader*, ed. Timothy Oakes and Patricia L. Price (London: Routledge, 2008). 337–45.

6

Concluding Remarks and Future Tasks

We have conducted a thoroughgoing analysis of Sustainable Finance based on empirical facts and discussed its philosophical grounds. The principal method employed is dialectics, as found in Hegel and Marx, above all Marx's method of proceeding from simple appearances to essence. Dialectics is a powerful tool that lifts the veil from the abstract and allows access to the concrete. Marx employs the Hegelian dialectic in *Grundrisse* and *Capital*; and this study, too, has approached Sustainable Finance from this perspective to reveal what lies behind the claims of the proponents of sustainability. Perhaps I should also refer to Hegel's Preface to the *Phenomenology of Spirit*. Indeed, his closing remarks on the work contain much insight into the dialectical approach. After working on this book did I understand Hegel's remarks in more concrete terms. When a work is complete, what is accomplished inevitably exceeds the initial goal. Since dialectics and the principle of immanence allow the topic to explain itself, the content can only be grasped at the end of the journey.

I explored sustainability in terms of its own historical development first. My analysis, especially in Chapter 2, showed that sustainability was initially linked to business ethics and corporate responsibility. The historical facts revealed that ESG first partly surfaced as a phenomenon in the late seventeenth century, mainly as a call for social responsibility in terms of investment. Religious sects sharply criticized money that was not utilized. Investment, therefore, was identified as a virtue—when ethically conducted.

Ecological and environmental concerns were raised very early on in history. However, simplifying a little, we can say that capitalist society overall has a double approach: if such concerns have a direct impact on profitability and growth, and if it is possible to defer them, capitalism prefers to disregard them. On the other hand, if such concerns become urgent and the current setup is no longer sustainable, then capitalism acts like the visionary that brought such concerns and proposals into the light. For instance, capitalism may have burned fossil fuels for centuries, disregarding criticisms of their use. However, now, in the midst of a climate crisis, it advocates for and even mandates a phase-out of coal. At the same time, however, exploiting this or that excuse, it can reverse its position, as we see in the increased use of coal during the war between Ukraine and Russia. Similarly, it promotes slogans about fighting climate change but quickly drops them if the fight harms profitability and growth. Capitalism is the system of abstract universality; the concrete always remains hidden.

Chapter 3 presents a long analysis of finance and Sustainable Finance. In this chapter, I benefited greatly from the third volume of Marx's *Capital*. A dialectical approach is used to analyze Sustainable Finance as a subcategory of finance as well as its evolution in relation to the latter and to capital overall. Every step of this analysis presents a negation of the determination of concepts presented by capitalist economy and society. Through this chain of negations, I demonstrate what lies behind the appearance of Sustainable Finance as a paradigm. The analysis reveals that the universal measure for managing capital allocation is the system of ratings. Ratings render almost all firms universal, telling us the amount of capital allocation, irrespective of where a firm is established. It is valid even for non-rated firms since, in order to have access to credit, they are also subject to such a standardized measure. A scenario was used to present the simple appearance of Sustainable Finance. In this scenario, a lender—typically, a bank—grants a loan to a firm. Upon the repayment of the loan, the bank accumulates money capital, and the firm will likely generate surplus value and profit, which it can add to its own capital. Thus, even though there is obviously a tension between money capital and industrial capital, the two have to work together to accumulate capital, despite money capital wanting independence. Money capital's independent nature, which means accumulation without production, constitutes the issue that we call financialization, which is further discussed in Chapter 4. Chapter 3 ends with the observation that profit is at the heart of both finance and Sustainable Finance. Capitalism would not survive without profit and growth, but by its very nature the system is vulnerable to crisis.

I discuss the limits and inadequacies of capitalism in Chapter 4. To make the matter concise and concrete, I elaborate on the basic tenets of Sustainable

Finance and the capitalist system in general. Chapter 4 starts with the net zero paradigm, which envisages a world free of GHG emissions by 2050. I point out that the decarbonization of the earth was also considered in the 1990s and failed. Capitalism now works according to its new paradigm for a decarbonized world by 2050. The past does not dictate the future; however, the capitalist system's immanent issues could easily lead to a deviation from efforts that make decarbonization hypothetically possible. Current flexibilities—or deviations—because of the Russo-Ukrainian war make it unlikely that firms will achieve net zero by 2050, although there is a real chance of success if a genuine commitment were to be made.

In Chapter 4, I also discuss the epistemological issues deriving from the structure of financial markets. Even an investor who does due diligence is vulnerable to the misrepresentation of financial assets in which to invest. Whatever may be written in textbooks and regulatory texts, there is no transparency in financial markets. Those who promote assets and generate them know their true nature while investors, especially small ones, struggle to grasp the truth with limited amounts of data and information. This makes the whole system a black hole that benefits only the big players. Thus, the growth and distribution of wealth remain unbalanced, making transparency immanently ambiguous and inaccessible to the larger population.

Chapter 4 also discusses neoliberal political economy. After the abandonment of the Keynesian economic model, deregulation in the financial system made the system even more vulnerable. It is not an exaggeration to say that the crises in the current capitalist system will be exclusively financial crises, as we saw in 2007–2009. We saw this again a few years ago when some hedge funds collapsed. And, very recently, with the collapse of the US Silicon Valley Bank, Signature Bank, and Credit Suisse in Switzerland. Financial regulators acted immediately to prevent a wider collapse, however. In any case, due to finance capital's unregulated nature and its immanent characteristics, the system will always be prone to such crises and vulnerabilities. The tension between deregulation and regulation is an oscillation between finance capital and industrial capital; however, the true problem lies at the very heart of the capitalist system.

Financialization is another major issue of the current capitalist system. Chapter 4 examines financialization in its relation to Sustainable Finance as well. Financialization makes capitalism a hegemonic power that includes both production and consumption. Even nature becomes a resource to be exploited.

Nature has a total value and is at the mercy of capital, even as capitalists promote a green planet by 2050. Growth and profitability, as well as financialization's expanded exploitation, are far from offering a green and sustainable planet. On the contrary, our planet is more vulnerable to the greediest members of our species—we should reflect again on whether our era should be called the Anthropocene or Capitalocene. Since Malthus claimed that food production would not satisfy the needs of a growing population, as Jacob Stevens puts it,[1] any egalitarian transformation of society was ruled out. Nonetheless, we need to seek egalitarian alternatives for a just transition that would solve the issue of sustainability and inequality.

Chapter 5 discusses the basic tenets of a better planet and sustainability. In this chapter, I employ the term "biopsychopolitics," which combines biopsychology and social psychology, as a companion to philosophy. I relate the term to Michel Foucault's biopolitics and Byung-Chul Han's psychopolitics, discussing their theoretical frameworks in detail. Biopsychopolitics sublates both their frameworks without any residue, since both are abstract: Foucault's is based exclusively on governmentality and gives a false interpretation of the art (!) of neoliberalism, while Han's separates psychology from biology.

Biopsychopolitics is presented in this study as the inauguration of a framework that can contribute to the Marxian framework. In order to make the matter more concise, I present two relatively brief examples to illustrate its application. The first concerns the ownership of the social means of production and demonstrates how inequality and discrimination negatively contribute to the class struggle and impact human beings in their relation to each other and to society. The second example concerns class consciousness and inequality. There have have several discussions of this topic. In the 1930s, the working class joined the totalitarian and fascist regimes. The reasons for this can be better understood through the study of the individual human psyche; on this basis, philosophy can reclaim its paradigm.

I was inspired by Herbert Marcuse in my work on biological-psychological matters. However, Marcuse's own inspiration was Freudian psychoanalysis, and I argue that social psychology and biopsychology are better elements, though not necessarily abolishing psychoanalysis.

Chapter 5 also discusses a new conception of class; or, rather, it recapitulates discussions. It does not propose a new definition. I refer to the broader account of class as explained by Domenico Losurdo, for instance. My purpose is to demonstrate that the tenets of orthodox Marxism contain little that would assist in changing society and the planet. Instead, I maintain that whatever is against capital forms part of the class struggle. This is not at all a rejection of Marx; it is simply a call to consider what Marx would think of our society today if he were here with us. It is absurd to rely on textual facts if their true context—their historical conditions—is not grasped. Hence, a new left should embrace all forces that oppose the world system. This should compose, at a very high level, an alliance that is a unity-in-difference. In this regard, I address the molecular politics of Gilles Deleuze—not to praise it, but as a counter to absurd interpretations of Marx.

What I find valuable in Deleuze's concept is that it provides a basis for resistance, especially at a time when the left has faced major defeats. However, it may be questionable whether their (Deleuze and Guattari's) concept of revolution can ever go beyond episodic or fragmented events. For example, when talking about the Radio Alice experience, Guattari claims that it was a revolution that would abolish not only capitalist systems but also the bureaucratic dictatorships of Beijing and Moscow.[2] History, for some good reason, has so far not justified these claims, since there is no guarantee that such sparks would spread and expand. Beyond these defeats, global capitalism has invaded almost every part of the planet, including its most depopulated areas from deep in the oceans up to the sky. If we do not accept this as a reality, we cannot understand the meaning and importance of molecular attempts that may—or may not—connect to molar transformations. This is a topic that should be discussed in detail by critical theory. If we do not focus on solutions, capitalism can deceive us, as, in my view, happens especially in the case of Žižek after the pandemic. According to Žižek, the role of the nation-state should be limited and subordinated to global initiatives. Without appropriate particulars, there can be no concrete universality. Despite his deep attention to abstract-concrete universalities, Žižek claims that NATO is to accord with European values, thus giving a master example of abstract universality, completely overlooking the role of US and European financial domination and the nature of NATO as the military vehicle of the Global North.[3] His use of communism is rather opportunistic; in his second book on Covid-19, he states that governments acted almost like communist states during the pandemic;[4] however, communism can easily be conflated with despotic or fascist regimes even when it provides needed remedies or measures if its ultimate societal form is ignored. I sometimes wonder what difference there would be between Žižek's brand of communism and Mussolini's 1919 Fascist Manifesto. Mussolini's manifesto included workers' rights, membership in trade unions, a minimum wage, and so on. By sticking to abstract facts, Žižek finds a way to mean several things at the same time. It is rather an art, one must admit. Contrary to his illusory statements, communism is not "one side of the coin";[5] on the contrary, there is an oscillation between latent despotism and Western democracy. Peter Osborne summarizes the dilemma of Žižek's approach well: "The mediating ground of the social—the structures and social forms of capitalist societies and the forms of collective practices they provoke, for example—is almost wholly absent."[6]

The sustainability of our planet is vital. It requires a reintegration of humans with nature, even as this integration reflects the abolition or the destruction of nature by humans as a species. Nonetheless, starting from an analysis of finance and Sustainable Finance, this study demonstrates that the current sustainability paradigm rests on growth and profitability. Sustainable Finance, beyond its appearance, differs from the sustainability of the planet. The term "sustainable" is an insufficient negation of the capitalist system: it declares that capitalism has not been sustainable *so far*. Contrary to its powerful and ubiquitous propaganda, sustainability mainly concerns the sustainability of capital. Sustainability means growth and profit ad infinitum. To strengthen this argument philosophically, I explore deregulation-regulation, financialization, and the net zero paradigm in detail. Capital first needs to be accumulated; then it should grow and bring more profit. Starting from an analysis of a simple transaction and following the path opened by Marx, I explain that commodities and their exchange always result in the accumulation of capital, which exploits the working class. This makes capitalist society and the capitalist economy intrinsically problematic.

Yet the capitalist system, though dominating societies and the world economy, nevertheless affords opportunities through its great technological innovations and advances. This is where *Aufhebung* plays an important conceptual role, one that needs to be actualized in practical struggle. Today, planning society's logistics and organization, and the ways to meet its needs, is perhaps easier than ever before. Today, we can easily identify which countries have a surplus and which countries lack food or energy. For this reason, abolishing capitalist society does not mean we should dispense with such gains. On the contrary, it means a better, possible society that preserves these advances and innovations. The same goes for finance. In the aftermath of the 2008 financial crisis, as we have witnessed on several occasions, the US financial system is better structured and controlled. This means that we can sublate the ownership of capital while maintaining finance's main contribution, as Matthew Lawrence and Laurie Laybourne-Langton put it.[7] This requires a drastic change to the world system: corporate and financial governance should ensure the fair and just distribution of wealth, resources, and funds for the fight against climate change.[8]

In the early 1970s, Marcuse emphasized the importance of nature in our struggle against exploitative societies. For him, the harm to nature was linked to the harm suffered by people, and nature was rediscovered as a partner in the struggle. Marcuse maintained that a novel driving force for social transformation was the liberating power of nature and its essential role in building a free society.[9] His prophetic statements were proved true in the following decades: ecology and the environment became an integral part of socialist resistance. Many of us are aware at some level that a better society is possible, although the capitalist worldview would have us believe otherwise. Marcuse employed the term "utopia" in this sense. For Marcuse, utopia is a possible reality. Ray Brassier argues[10] that even the domain of possibility has been taken over by capitalism. This is true; I imagine the spread of capitalism as plasma covering the planet, the fauna, the flora, nobody able to perceive it since it is transparent and gossamer-like. Our lives are completely occupied. Due to the impact of finance capitalism, not only are we exploited and alienated in our working hours, but control and domination extend into our daily lives. Besides Adorno and Horkheimer's culture industry, we are held captive by mortgages, credit cards, and everything that pledges our future to the system. So, the problem is rather atomization than complacency.

For a long time, I've believed that rejecting dialectics is like rejecting life's natural progression. Dialectics represents life's processes, though it has been imperfectly executed historically. For instance, saying "dialectical process" is redundant since dialectics implies a process already. The challenge lies in how much the dialectic in life (social, personal, etc.) coincides with intellectual dialectics. The events and perpetual changes in life don't always align with intellectual discourse. The mathematical principle where two negatives equal a positive doesn't apply here. Recognizing this duality could have been more productive; despite numerous discussions around this theme, they often go unaddressed.

Adorno credits Hegel's insights with enabling contemporary social theory and acknowledges Hegel's pivotal role in transforming perceptions of history and social structures, moving beyond the notion of an isolated individual. However, Hegel also faces a major contradiction: he ascribes all negation and change to achieving a predestined end. In this view, reason comes full circle, returning to its origin to realize itself. Although Žižek points out this retrospective teleological aspect in Hegel, it is hard to defend it on a naturalist or materialist basis. Hegel seems to attempt a fusion of contrasting philosophical Greek ideas about the universe's inertia and perpetual motion. Yet, this attempt surfaces as his weakness because eventually, all institutional negation within his teleological idealism turns into positivism, counteracting dialectics' very nature—akin to idealism's predictable finality in various forms.

Another major problem with the concept of progressive and self-actualizing reason in history is its conflict with particularity. Although Hegel is credited by some thinkers with a good synthesis of the universal and the particular, it seems that his view contains an internal conflict. His own thought represents the universal, and in every conflict resolved by Hegelian dialectics, it signifies, on the other hand, the subjugation of resistance and its dissolution into the dominant universal. This is a historical fact, but it is not something we should be proud of; in fact, it represents our ruined nature and destroyed life.

Concept and object cannot be identical, and a complete union between subject and object isn't possible; a division always remains. Defending Hegel also requires abandoning some Hegelian principles. Perhaps embracing an open-ended negation aligns better with understanding life. Instead of claiming to unearth universal truths, recognizing and trying to bridge the divide between life's flow and our comprehension is both accurate and ethical. The focus should be on cognition and striving to close this gap. Grand assertions have consistently signaled the onset of social and personal calamities.

The question that we first need to ask is whether utopia is what we need; then, how a practice to radically transform society can become possible again. I conclude with my belief that a better society is still possible—yet must be justified and actualized!

Notes

1 Jacob Stevens, "The Monetized Ecology," *New Left Review* 16 (July-August 2002): 143–51.

2 Félix Guattari, *Molecular Revolution: Psychiatry and Politics* (London: Penguin, 1984), 240.

3 Slavoj Žižek, "Pacifism is the Wrong Response to the War in Ukraine," *The Guardian*, June 21, 2022. https://www.theguardian.com/commentisfree/2022/jun/21/pacificsm-is-the-wrong-response-to-the-war-in-ukraine.

4 Slavoj Žižek, *Pandemic! 2: Chronicles of a Time Lost* (New York and London: OR Books, 2020), 28.

5 Ibid., 29.

6 Peter Osborne, "'More than everything': Žižek's Badiouian Hegel," *Radical Philosophy* 177 (2013): 19–25.

7 Mathew Lawrence and Laurie Laybourn-Langton, *Planet on Fire: A Manifesto for the Age of Environmental Breakdown* (London: Verso, 2021), 113. The authors stress that the democratization of finance is essential to the Green New Deal so that social control can be established.

8 Chris Saltmarsh, *Burnt* (London: Pluto Press, 2021), 46.

9 Herbert Marcuse, *Counterrevolution and Revolt* (New York: Beacon Press, 1972), 59.

10 Ray Brassier, "Introduction," in Marcuse, *Psychoanalysis, Politics, and Utopia*, 1.

Bibliography

Adorno, Theodor W. *An Introduction to Dialectics*. Edited by Christoph Ziermann. Translated by Nicholas Walker. London: Polity, 2017.

Adorno, Theodor W. *History and Freedom*. Edited by Rolf Tiedemann. Translated by Rodney Livingstone. London: Polity, 2006.

Adorno, Theodor W. *Lectures on Negative Dialectics*. Edited by Rolf Tiedemann. Translated by Rodney Livingstone. London: Polity, 2008.

Adorno, Theodor W. *Minima Moralia: Reflections From Damaged Life*. Translated by E. F. N. Jephcott. London: Verso, 2005.

Adorno, Theodor W. *Ontology and Dialectics*. Edited by Rolf Tiedemann. Translated by Nicholas Walker. London: Polity, 2019.

Adorno, Theodor W. *Philosophy of Modern Music*. Translated by Anne G. Mitchell and Wesley V. Blomster. London: Bloomsbury, 2017.

Adorno, Theodor W. *Problems of Moral Philosophy*. Edited by Thomas Schröder. Translated by Rodney Livingstone. London: Polity, 2000.

Ajl, Max. *A People's New Green Deal*. London: Pluto Press, 2021.

Akepa. "Greenwashing: 11 Recent Stand-out Examples." July 23, 2021. https://thesustainableagency.com/blog/greenwashing-examples/.

Angus, Ian. *Facing the Anthropocene: Fossil Capitalism and the Crisis of the Earth System*. New York: Monthly Review Press, 2016.

Aqeel, Hisham. "Visiting Hegel at Dusk: A Conversation with Slavoj Žižek." *Rethinking Marxism* 32, no. 4 (2020): 459–66.

Aronoff, Kate. "Recharging Internationalism." In *A Planet to Win: Why We Need a Green New Deal,* edited by Kate Aronoff, Alyssa Battistoni, Daniel Aldana Cohen, and Thea Riafrancos. London and New York: Verso, 2019.

Aronson, Elliot, Timothy D. Wilson, and Samuel R. Sommers. *Social Psychology*. 10th ed. London: Pearson, 2019.

Badiou, Alain. *Ethics: An Essay on the Understanding of Evil*. Translated by Peter Hallward. London: Verso, 2001.

Bahro, Rudolf. *From Red to Green*. Translated by Gus Fagan and Richard Hurst. London: Verso, 1984.

Baldarelli, Maria-Gabriella, Mara Del Baldo, and Caterina Ferrone. "The Relationships between CSR, Good Governance and Accountability in the Economy of Communion (EoC) Enterprises." In *Corporate Social Responsibility and Governance: Theory and Practice*, edited by Samuel O. Idowu, Claus Strue Frederiksen, Asli Yüksel, and Morten Ebe Juul Nielsen. London: Springer, 2015.

Bank for International Settlements. "Basel Committee on Banking Supervision: CRE Calculation of RWA for Credit Risk. CRE 20. Standardised Approach: Individual Exposures." Version effective as of January 1, 2023.

Baudrillard, Jean. *Simulacra and Simulation*. Translated by Sheila Faria Glaser. Michigan: The Michigan University Press, 1994.

BBC. "COP26: What was Agreed at the Glasgow Climate Conference?" *BBC*, November 15, 2021.

Berrou, Romain, Nicola Ciampoli, and Vladimiro Marini. "Defining Green Finance: Existing Standards and Main Challenges." In *The Rise of Green Finance in Europe*, edited by Marco Migliorelli and Philippe Dessertine. Cham: Palgrave Macmillan, 2019.

Bhaskar, Roy. *Dialectic: The Pulse of Freedom*. New York: Routledge, 2008.

Bhaskar, Roy. *Enlighted Common Sense: The Philosophy of Critical Realism*. New York: Routledge, 2016.

Bloomberg. "ESG May Surpass $41 Trillion Assets in 2022, But Not Without Challenges, Finds Bloomberg Intelligence." *Bloomberg*, January 24, 2022.

Bookchin, Murray. *The Ecology of Freedom: The Emergence and Dissolution of Hierarchy*. Montreal: Black Rose Books, 1991.

Boyle, Louise and Saphora Smith. "Cop27 Outcomes: Key Takeaways from the Final Agreement." *The Independent,* November 21, 2022.

Brassier, Ray. Introduction to *Psychoanalysis, Politics, and Utopia: Five Lectures.* Edited by Herbert Marcuse, 1–12. London: Repeater Books, 2022.

Buck, Holly Jean. *Ending Fossil Fuels: Why Net Zero is Not Enough.* London: Verso, 2021.

Burbidge, John W. *Historical Dictionary of Hegelian Philosophy*. Lanham, MD, Toronto, Plymouth: The Scarecrow Press, 2008.

Cadbury, Henry J. "Another early Quaker Anti-slavery Document." *The Journal of Negro History* 27, no. 2 (1942): 210–15.

Carbon Disclosure Project. "Finance Sector's Funded Emissions over 700 Times Greater than its Own." *CDP*, April 28, 2021.

Carroll, Archie B. "Corporate Social Responsibility (CSR) and the COVID-19 Pandemic: Organizational and Managerial Implications." *Journal of Strategy and Management* 14, no. 3 (2021): 315–30.

Carson, Rachel. *Silent Spring*. Boston: Mariner Books, 2002.

Carvacho, Hector and Belen Alvarez. "Inequality and Class Consciousness." In *The Social Psychology of Inequality*, edited by Jolanda Jetten and Kim Peters. New York: Springer, 2019.

Cebada, Juan Diego Perez. "An Editorial Flop Revisited: Rethinking the Impact of Murray Bookchin's Our Synthetic Environment on its Golden Anniversary." *Global Environment: A Journal of Transdisciplinary History* 6, no. 12 (2013): 250–73.

Chandler, Chris. *Psychobiology*. West Sussex: John Wiley & Sons, 2015.

Chomsky, Noam and Robert Pollin. *Climate Crisis and the Global Green New Deal.* London and New York: Verso, 2020.

CNBC. "Germany's Increased Coil, Oil Use will be Temporary, Scholz says." *CNBC*, July 16, 2022.

CNN. "US Aid to Israel and Ukraine: Here's what's in the $105 billion National Security Package Biden Requested." November 28, 2023.

Commoner, Barry. *The Closing Circle: Nature, Man, and Technology*. New York: Alfred A. Knopf, 1971.

Crandall, Christian S., and Amy Eshleman. "A Justification-suppression Model of the Expression and Experience of Prejudice." *Psychological Bulletin* 129, no. 3 (2003): 414–46.

Cresswell, Tim. "The Production of Mobilities." In *The Cultural Geography Reader*, edited by Timothy Oakes and Patricia L. Price. New York: Routledge, 2008.

Dahlquist, Julie and Rainford Knight. *Principles of Finance*. Houston, TX: OpenStax, 2022.

Deleuze, Gilles and Felix Guattari. *A Thousand Plateaus: Capitalism and Schizophrenia*. Translated by Brian Massumi. Minneapolis and London: University of Minnesota Press, 1987.

Deutsche Welle. "Germany Commits €100 billion to Defense Spending." *Deutsche Welle*, February 27, 2022.

Dillinger, Jessica. "The Top 10 Coal Producers Worldwide." *WorldAtlas*, June 14, 2020. https://www.worldatlas.com/articles/the-top-10-coal-producers-worldwide.html.

Dimitrova, Maria. *Sociality and Justice: Toward Social Phenomenology*. Stuttgart: Ibidem, 2016.

Dobbs, Richard and Michael Spence. "The Era of Cheap Capital Draws to a Close." *McKinsey*, February 1, 2011. https://www.mckinsey.com/featured-insights/employment-and-growth/the-era-of-cheap-capital-draws-to-a-close.

Durand, Cédric. *Fictitious Capital: How Finance is Appropriating Our Future.* Translated by David Broder. London: Verso, 2017.

Dyke, James, Robert Watson, and Wolfgang Knorr. "Climate Scientists: Concept of Net Zero is a Dangerous Trap." *The Conversation*, April 22, 2021.

Eckert, Vera and Tom Sims. "Energy Crisis Fuels Coal Comeback in Germany." *Reuters*, December 16, 2022.

Elkington, John. "The Triple Bottom Line." *Environment Management: Readings and Cases* 2 (1997): 49–66.

Engels, Friedrich. *Karl Marx, Frederick Engels: Collected Works, Vol. 4, Marx and Engels: 1844-1845.* London: Lawrence & Wishart, 1975.

Engels, Friedrich. *Karl Marx, Frederick Engels: Collected Works, Vol. 5, Marx and Engels: 1845-1847.* London: Lawrence & Wishart, 1976

Engels, Friedrich. *Karl Marx, Frederick Engels: Collected Works, Vol. 21, Marx and Engels: 1867-1870.* London: Lawrence & Wishart, 2001.

Engels, Friedrich. *Karl Marx, Frederick Engels: Collected Works, Vol. 25, Engels: 1873-1883.* London: Lawrence & Wishart, 1987.

Engels, Friedrich. *Karl Marx, Frederick Engels: Collected Works, Vol. 26, Engels: 1882-1889.* New York: International Publishers, 1990.

Engels, Friedrich. *Karl Marx, Frederick Engels: Collected Works, Vol. 42, Marx and Engels: 1864-1868.* London: Lawrence & Wishart, 1987.

Engels, Friedrich. *Karl Marx, Frederick Engels: Collected Works, Vol. 43, Marx and Engels: 1868-1870.* London: Lawrence & Wishart, 2001.

Engels, Friedrich. *Karl Marx, Frederick Engels: Collected Works, Vol. 49, Letters: 1890-1892.* London: Lawrence & Wishart, 2001.

Environment Justice Atlas. "Groundwater Contamination with Chromium-6 in Hinkley, California." *EJ Atlas*, April 9, 2018.

Fine, Ben and Alfredo Saad-Filho. *Marx's Capital*. 5th ed. London: Pluto Press, 2010.

Fisher, Mark. *Capitalist Realism: Is There No Alternative?* London: Zero Books, 2009.

Foster, John Bellamy. *Marx's Ecology: Materialism and Nature.* New York: Monthly Review Press, 2000.

Foster, John Bellamy. "Nature as a Mode of Accumulation." *Monthly Review*, March 1, 2022.

Foster, John Bellamy. *The Vulnerable Planet: A Short Economic History of the Environment*. New York: Monthly Review Press, 1999.

Foucault, Michel. *The Birth of Biopolitics: Lectures at the Collège de France 1978–1979.* Edited by Michel Senellart. Translated by Graham Burchell. London: Palgrave Macmillan, 2009.

Foucault, Michel. *The History of Sexuality, Volume 1: Introduction*. Translated by Robert Hurley. New York: Pantheon Books, 1978.

Foucault, Michel. *Security, Territory, and Population: Lectures at the Collège de France 1977–1978*. Edited by Michel Senellart. Translated by Graham Burchell. London: Palgrave Macmillan, 2007.

Foucault, Michel. *Society Must be Defended: Lectures at the Collège de France 1975–1976*. Edited by Mauro Bertani and Alessandro Fontana. Translated by David Macey. London: Picador, 2003.

Foucault, Michel. "What Is Enlightenment?" In *Ethics: Subjectivity and Truth, Essential Works of Foucault 1954–1984*, vol. 1, edited by Paul Rabinow, translated by Catherine Porter (revised). New York and London: The New Press, 2003.

Fraas, Karl N. *Klima und Pflanzenwelt in der Zeit, ein Beitrag zur Geschichte Beider.* Landshut: J. G. Wölfe, 1847.

Friends of the Earth International. "COP27 Outcome: Loss and Damage Fund Established in Historic First Step, but Other Outcomes Perilously Weak." *FOEI*, November 20, 2022.

Guattari, Felix. *Molecular Revolution: Psychiatry and Politics*. London: Penguin, 1984.

Gorz, André. *Ecology as Politics*. Translated by Patsy Vigderman and Jonathan Cloud. Boston: South End Press, 1980.

Han, Byung-Chul. *Psychopolitics: Neoliberalism and New Technologies of Power*. Translated by Erik Butler. London: Verso, 2017.

Harrabin, Roger. "Paris Agreement: Trump Confirms US will Leave Climate Accord." *BBC*, October 24, 2019. https://www.bbc.com/news/world-us-canada-50165596.

Harvey, David. *A Companion to Marx's Capital: The Complete Edition*. London: Verso, 2018.

Harvey, David. *Spaces of Global Capitalism: Towards a Theory of Uneven Geographical Development*. London: Verso, 2006.

Harvey, David. *The Limits to Capital*. London: Verso Books, 2018.

Hegel, Georg Friedrich Wilhelm. *The Encyclopaedia Logic*. Translated by T. F. Geraets, W. A. Suchting, and H. S. Harris. Indianapolis and Cambridge: Hackett Publishing Company, Inc., 1991.

Hegel, Georg Friedrich Wilhelm. *Hegel: Philosophy of Mind*. Translated by W. Wallace and A. V. Miller, revised by Michael Inwood. Oxford: Oxford University Press, 2010.

Hegel, Georg Friedrich Wilhelm. *Lectures on Logic: Berlin, 1831*. Translated by Clark Butler. Bloomington and Indianapolis: Indiana University Press, 2008.

Hegel, Georg Friedrich Wilhelm. *The Phenomenology of Spirit*. Translated by Michael Inwood. Oxford: Oxford University Press, 2018.

Hegel, Georg Friedrich Wilhelm. *The Science of Logic*. Edited and translated by George di Giovanni. Cambridge: Cambridge University Press, 2010.

Herber, Lewis. "The Problem of Chemicals in Food." *Contemporary Issues: A Magazine for a Democracy of Content* 3, no. 12 (1952): 206–41.

Herrera, M. Carmen, Francisca Expósito, and Miguel Moya. "Negative Reactions of Men to the Loss of Power in Gender Relations: Lilith vs. Eve." *The European Journal of Psychology Applied to Legal Context* 4, no. 1 (2012): 17–42.

Hess, Peter N. *Economic Growth and Sustainable Development*. New York: Routledge, 2013.

Horkheimer, Max. *Dawn & Decline: Notes 1926-1931 and 1950-1969*. Translated by Michael Shaw. New York: The Seabury Press, 1978.

Hornborg, Alf. "Ecological Economics, Marxism, and Technological Progress: Some Explorations of the Conceptual Foundations of Theories of Ecologically Unequal Exchange." *Ecological Economics* 105 (2014): 11–18.

Huber, Matthew T. *Climate Change as Class War: Building Socialism on a Warming Planet*. London: Verso, 2022.

Hunt, Colin. "Kyoto Protocol Fails: Get Ready for a Hotter World." *The Conversation*, November 16, 2012.

Kalat, James W. *Biological Psychology*. 13th ed. Boston: Cengage, 2019.

Kaufman, Leeor and Joe Egender, dir. "Changing an Entire Species." In Unnatural Selection. Netflix, 2019. https://www.netflix.com/watch/80208835

Keynes, John Maynard. *A Treatise on Money, Volume 1: The Pure Theory of Money*. Cambridge: Cambridge University Press, 2013.

Keynes, John Maynard. *A Treatise on Money, Volume 2: The Applied Theory of Money*. Cambridge: Cambridge University Press, 2013.

Keynes, John Maynard. *The General Theory of Employment, Interest and Money*. Cham: Palgrave Macmillan, 2018.

Knight, Ben. "Where is Germany's Military Budget Going?" *Deutsche Welle*, March 18, 2022.

Kojève, Alexandre. *Introduction to the Reading of Hegel: Lectures on the Phenomenology of Spirit*. Translated by James H. Nichols, Jr. Ithaca and London: Cornell University Press, 1980.

Kruttli, Mathias S., Phillip J. Monin, Lubomir Petrasek, and Sumudu W. Watugala. "Hedge Fund Treasury Trading and Funding Fragility: Evidence from the COVID-19 Crisis." Finance and Economics Discussion Series 2021-038 (Washington: Board of Governors of the Federal Reserve System), https://doi.org/10.17016/FEDS.2021.038.

Lamb, Peter. *Marx and Engels' "Communist Manifesto": A Reader's Guide*. London and New York: Bloomsbury Academic, 2015.

Lapavitsas, Costas. *Profiting Without Producing: How Finance Exploits Us All*. London and New York: Verso Books, 2013.

Lapavitsas, Costas. "Theorizing Financialization." *Work, Employment and Society* 25, no. 4 (2011): 611–26.

Lawrence, Mathew and Laurie Laybourn-Langton. *Planet on Fire: A Manifesto for the Age of Environmental Breakdown*. London: Verso, 2021.

Leeson, Niam. *Rogue Trader: How I Brought Down Barings Bank and Shook the Financial World*. Boston: Little, Brown & Company, 1996.

Levinas, Emmanuel. *Otherwise Than Being or Beyond Essence*. Translated by Alphonso Lingis. Pittsburgh: Duquesne University Press, 1998.

Losurdo, Domenico. *Class Struggle: A Political and Philosophical History*. London: Palgrave Macmillan, 2016.

Luxemburg, Rosa. *The Russian Revolution and Leninism or Marxism*. Ann Arbor: University of Michigan Press, 1961.

Lyotard, Jean-François. *Why Philosophize?* Translated by Andrew Brown. London: Polity, 2013.

Magee, Glenn Alexander. *The Hegel Dictionary*. London and New York: Continuum, 2010.

Mallin, Christine A. "Introduction and Overview." In *Corporate Social Responsibility: A Case Study Approach*, edited by Christine A. Mallin. Northampton, MA: Edward Elgar, 2009.

Mamardashvili, Merab. "Converted Forms: On the Need for Irrational Expressions." *Stasis* 5 (2017): 204–17.

Marcuse, Herbert. *Counterrevolution and Revolt*. Boston: Beacon Press, 2010.

Marcuse, Herbert. *Hegel's Ontology and the Theory of Historicity*. Translated by Seyla Benhabib. Cambridge, MA: MIT Press, 1987.

Marcuse, Herbert. *Psychoanalysis, Politics, and Utopia: Five Lectures*. Edited by Ray Brassier. Translated by Jeremy J. Shapiro and Shierry M. Weber. London: Repeater Books, 2022.

Marcuse, Herbert. *Reason and Revolution: Hegel and the Rise of Social Theory*. London and New York: Routledge, 2000.

Marcuse, Herbert. *Towards a Critical Theory of Society*. London and New York: Routledge, 2001.

Marx, Karl. *A Contribution to the Critique of Political Economy*. Translated by N. I. Stone. Chicago: Charles H. Kerr & Company, 1904.

Marx, Karl. *Capital: A Critique of Political Economy*, Vol. 1. Translated by Ben Fowkes. London: Penguin, 1990.

Marx, Karl. *Capital: A Critique of Political Economy*, Vol. 3. Translated by David Fernbach. London: Penguin, 1991.

Marx, Karl. *Karl Marx, Frederick Engels: Collected Works, Vol. 5, Marx and Engels: 1845-1847*. London: Lawrence & Wishart, 1975.

Marx, Karl. *Karl Marx, Frederick Engels: Collected Works, Vol. 12, Marx and Engels: 1853-1854*. London: Lawrence & Wishart, 1976.

Marx, Karl. *Karl Marx, Frederick Engels: Collected Works, Vol. 40, Marx and Engels: 1856-1859*. London: Lawrence & Wishart, 1983.

Marx, Karl. *Karl Marx, Frederick Engels: Collected Works, Vol. 42, Marx and Engels: 1864-1868*. London: Lawrence & Wishart, 1987.

Marx, Karl. *Karl Marx, Frederick Engels: Collected Works, Vol. 43, Marx and Engels: 1868-1870*. London: Lawrence & Wishart, 1983.

Marx, Karl. *Theories of Surplus-Value: Volume IV of Capital*, Part III. Translated by G. A. Bonner and Emile Burns. Moscow: Progress Publishers, 1971.

Marx, Karl and Friedrich Engels. *The Communist Manifesto*. Translated by Samuel Moore. New York and London: W. W. Norton & Company, 1988.

Marx, Karl and Friedrich Engels. *The German Ideology*. New York: Prometheus Books, 1998.

Mathiesen, Karl and Zia Weise. "Greta Thunberg calls Germany Using Coal over Nuclear a 'Bad Idea.'" *Politico*, October 11, 2022.

McKenna, Tony. "Against Post-Marxism: How Post-Marxism Annuls Class-Based Historicism and the Possibility of Revolutionary Praxis." *International Critical Thought* 4 (2014): 142–59.

McKinsey. "What is Net Zero?" November 28, 2022. https://www.mckinsey.com/featured-insights/mckinsey-explainers/what-is-net-zero.

Meaney, Mark E. *Capital as Organic Unity: The Role of Hegel's Science of Logic in Marx's Grundrisse*. Dordrecht: Springer, 2002.

Means, Alexander J. "Foucault, Biopolitics, and the Critique of State Reason." *Educational Philosophy and Theory* 54, no. 12 (2023): 1–2.

Melis Andrea, Silvia Carta, and Silvia Del Rio. "CSR and Integrated Triple Bottom Line Reporting in Italy." In *Corporate Social Responsibility: A Case Study Approach*, edited by Christine A. Mallin. Northampton, MA: Edward Elgar, 2009.

Moseley Fred et al. *Marx's Capital and Hegel's Logic: A Reexamination*. Leiden: Brill, 2016.

Nelson, Eric S. *Levinas, Adorno, and the Ethics of the Material Other*. New York: State University of New York Press, 2020.

Network for Greening the Financial System. "About Us." https://www.ngfs.net/ngfs-scenarios-portal/about/.

Net-Zero Banking Alliance. "Our Members." Updated July 14, 2024. https://www.unepfi.org/net-zero-banking/members/.

Norrie, Alan. *Dialectic and Difference: Dialectical Critical Realism and the Grounds of Justice*. New York: Routledge, 2010.

Osborne, Peter. "More than everything: Žižek's Badiouian Hegel." *Radical Philosophy* 177 (January/February 2013): 19–25.

Ott, Julia C. *When Wall Street Met Main Street*. Cambridge, MA: Harvard University Press, 2011.

Palley, Thomas I. "Financialization: What It Is and Why It Matters." The Levy Economics Institute of Bard College Working Paper No. 525, December 2007. https://www.levyinstitute.org/pubs/wp_525.pdf.

Pearl, Mike. "The Town Erin Brockovich Rescued is Basically a Ghost Town Now." *Vice*, April 15, 2015.

Pickett, Kate and Richard Wilkinson. *The Spirit Level: Why Equality is Better for Everyone*. London: Penguin, 2010.

Piketty, Thomas. *Capital and Ideology*. Translated by Arthur Goldhammer. Cambridge, MA and London: The Belknap Press of Harvard University Press, 2020.

Pinel, P. J. and Steven J. Barnes. *Biopsychology*. 11th ed. London: Pearson, 2022.

Pollin, Robert. "The Man Who Explained Empire: Remembering Harry Magdoff." *Counterpunch*, January 6, 2006.

Pollin, Robert. "Remembering Paul Sweezy: 'He was an Amazingly Great Man.'" *Counterpunch*, March 6-7, 2004.

Reuters. "Britain to Keep Coal-fired Power Plants Open this Winter." *Reuters*, July 29, 2022.

Riotta, Chris. "Trump Repeats False Claim there is No Climate Change Crisis as he Brands Science 'Fake.'" *The Independent*, March 12, 2019.

Rockhill, Gabriel. "Foucault: The Faux Radical." *The Philosophical Salon*, October 12, 2020.

Rosen, Stanley. *The Idea of Hegel's Science of Logic*. Chicago: University of Chicago Press, 2014.

Rowling, Megan. "Analysis: COP27 Loss and Damage Fund Heralds 'New Dawn for Climate Justice.'" *Reuters*, November 20, 2022.

Sachs, Jeffrey. *The End of Poverty: Economic Possibilities for Our Time*. London: Penguin, 2005.

Saltmarsh, Chris. *Burnt*. London: Pluto Press, 2021.

Sawyer, Malcolm. "What is Financialization?" *International Journal of Political Economy*, 42, no. 4 (Winter 2013-14): 5–18.

Schmitz, Rob. "Amid an Energy Crisis, Germany Turns to the World's Dirtiest Fossil Fuel." *NPR*, September 27, 2022.

Schrimpf, Andreas, Hyun Song Shin, and Vladyslav Sushko, "Leverage and Margin Spirals in Fixed Income Markets during the COVID-19 Crisis." *BIS Bulletin* no. 2, Bank for International Settlement, April 2, 2020.

See-Yan, Lee. "Chairman's Summary and Recommendations." In *Finance for Sustainable Development: Testing New Policy Approaches*, edited by Juergen Holst, Donald Lee, and Eric Olson. New York: United Nations, 2002.

Shaw, Christopher W. *Money, Power and the People*. Chicago: University of Chicago Press, 2019.

Simmel, Georg. *The Philosophy of Money*. Translated by Tom Bottomore and David Frisby. London: Routledge, 2011.

Stevens, Jacob. "The Monetized Ecology." *New Left Review* 16 (July-August 2002): 143–51.

Sustainalytics. *Company ESG Risks: The Coca-Cola Co*. https://www.sustainalytics .com/esg-rating/coca-cola-consolidated-inc/1008405059.

Uchida, Hiroshi. *Marx's Grundrisse and Hegel's Logic*. London: Routledge, 1988.

United Nations. "The 17 Goals." Updated April 10, 2022. https://sdgs.un.org/goals.

United Nations. "The Millennium Development Goals Report 2015." July 2015. http://mdgs.un.org/unsd/mdg/Resources/Static/Products/Progress2015/English2015.pdf.

United Nations Environment Programme. "Definitions and Concepts: Background Note." Inquiry Working Paper 16/13, New York. September 2016.

United Nations Environment Programme Finance Initiative. "A Legal Framework for Impact: Sustainability Impact in Investor Decision-making." July 2021. https://www.unepfi.org/publications/a-legal-framework-for-impact-sustainability-impact-in-investor-decision-making/.

United Nations Environment Programme Finance Initiative. "From 1992 to 2021: The Evolution of Sustainable Finance." June 2017. https://www.unepfi.org/news/25th-anniversary/timeline/.

United Nations Environment Programme Finance Initiative. "Guidelines for Climate Target Setting for Banks." April 2021. https://www.unepfi.org/wordpress/wp-content/uploads/2021/04/UNEP-FI-Guidelines-for-Climate-Change-Target-Setting.pdf.

United Nations Environment Programme Finance Initiative. "Rethinking Impact to Finance the SDGs: A Position Paper and Call to Action Prepared by Positive Impact Initiative." November 2018. https://www.unepfi.org/wordpress/wp-content/uploads/2018/11/Rethinking-Impact-to-Finance-the-SDGs.pdf.

United Nations Environment Programme Finance Initiative. "Testing the Application of the EU Taxonomy to Core Banking Products: High Level Recommendations." January 2021. https://www.unepfi.org/industries/banking/eu-taxonomy-testing-core-banking-products/.

United Nations Environment Programme Finance Initiative. "Turning the Tide: How to Finance a Sustainable Ocean Recovery." March 2021. https://www.unepfi.org/publications/turning-the-tide/.

United Nations Framework Convention on Climate Change. "CEO Briefing on Climate Change." August 2002. https://www.unepfi.org/fileadmin/documents/CEO_briefing_climate_change_2002_en.pdf.

United Nations Framework Convention on Climate Change. "Paris Agreement." 2015. https://unfccc.int/sites/default/files/english_paris_agreement.pdf.

United Nations Framework Convention on Climate Change. "Summary of Global Climate Action at COP28 – UNFCC." https://unfccc.int/sites/default/files/resource/Summary_GCA_COP28.pdf.

Verene, Donald Phillip. *An Introduction to Reading the Phenomenology of Spirit*. Albany: State University of New York Press, 2007

Waring, Bonnie. "There aren't Enough Trees in the World to Offset Society's Carbon Emissions – And there Never will be." *The Conversation*, April 23, 2021.

Wesley, John. *The Works of John Wesley, Vol.6, First Series of Sermons (40-53) Second Series Begun (54-86)*. Albany: Books For The Ages, 1997.

Wilkins, Brett. "Climate Scientists: 'Net Zero' is a Dangerous Trap." *Climate and Capitalism*, April 22, 2021.

Wood, Ellen Meiksins. *The Origin of Capitalism: A Longer View.* London: Verso, 2017.

World Economic Forum. "COP28 Agrees to Establish Loss and Damage Fund for Vulnerable Countries." December 1, 2023. https://www.weforum.org/agenda/2023/12/cop28-loss-and-damage-fund-climate-change/.

Žižek, Slavoj. *Hegel in a Wired Brain*. London: Bloomsbury, 2020.

Žižek, Slavoj. "Pacifism is the Wrong Response to the War in Ukraine." *The Guardian*, June 21, 2022.

Žižek, Slavoj. *Pandemic! 2: Chronicles of a Time Lost*. New York and London: OR Books, 2020.

Index

Note: Page numbers followed by 'n' denotes note numbers

www.ingramcontent.com/pod-product-compliance
Ingram Content Group UK Ltd.
Pitfield, Milton Keynes, MK11 3LW, UK
UKHW021030041026
15470UKWH00013B/1247